CHOICES
Workbook

HOW TO MEND OR END
A BROKEN RELATIONSHIP

LAUREN S. CLUCAS

INGENIUM BOOKS

ISBNS
eBook: 978-1-990688-12-6
Paperback: 978-1-990688-11-9

ABOUT THE PUBLISHER
Ingenium Books Publishing Inc.
Toronto, Ontario, Canada M6P 1Z2
ingeniumbooks.com

Editing by Boni Wagner-Stafford
Typeset by Amie McCracken
Cover design by Jessica Bell Design

Contents

INTRODUCTION

Welcome to *Choices: How to Mend or End a Broken Relationship* (*The Workbook*). Congratulations on being committed to working through your relationship challenges in an applied way and to the beginning of a new, better relationship with yourself.

This workbook is designed to be your personal resource and used in tandem with the main book. If you have purchased this workbook without also purchasing the main book, stop now and be sure you have both! You can find the main book here: ingeniumbooks.com/CHCS

Here you'll find the exercises organized in the same order as the relevant chapters in the main *Choices* book so you can follow along or refer back to the main copy for the meat on each topic. You can keep your answers for your own records so that you can track your patterns and growth.

You might work through on your own, together with your partner, or select certain exercises that both you and your partner complete and then discuss. Either way, I hope you enjoy doing the work and relish the opportunity of getting to know yourself that much better!

1 ATTACHMENT STYLES

• Do you recall the level of attentiveness you were shown as a child by way of touch, empathy, and presence of your mother and father? Record your recollections below.

_____

_____

_____

• Do you know what attachment style you bring to your relationships? Review the list of attachment styles in chapter 6, "Becoming Attached," and make note of this style and why you believe it applies to you.

_____

_____

_____

• Do you understand how your hardwiring could be affecting your degree of reactivity, and do you get triggered without understanding why? Explore and explain.

_____

_____

_____

- Do you have predisposed views of men/women/relationships that have you sabotaging yourself? Write down these views and also some examples of ways you sabotage yourself as a result.

- Do you have a fear of intimacy yet yearn for it at the same time? Why might you fear intimacy? Why do you yearn for it?

- Do your partners tell you that you give mixed messages or that you come across as ambivalent? When has this happened? What were the mixed messages about? Why do you think this occurred?

- Do you find yourself constantly seeking reassurance from your partner? In what ways? When, and why?

- Do you test your partner with games and threats to leave or attempt to make them jealous? Explain.

_____

_____

_____

- Do you fear being controlled, fear being loved, and fear losing your independence? Record your answers and attempt to explain for yourself and your partner why this might be.

_____

_____

_____

_____

_____

_____

_____

_____

_____

_____

_____

_____

_____

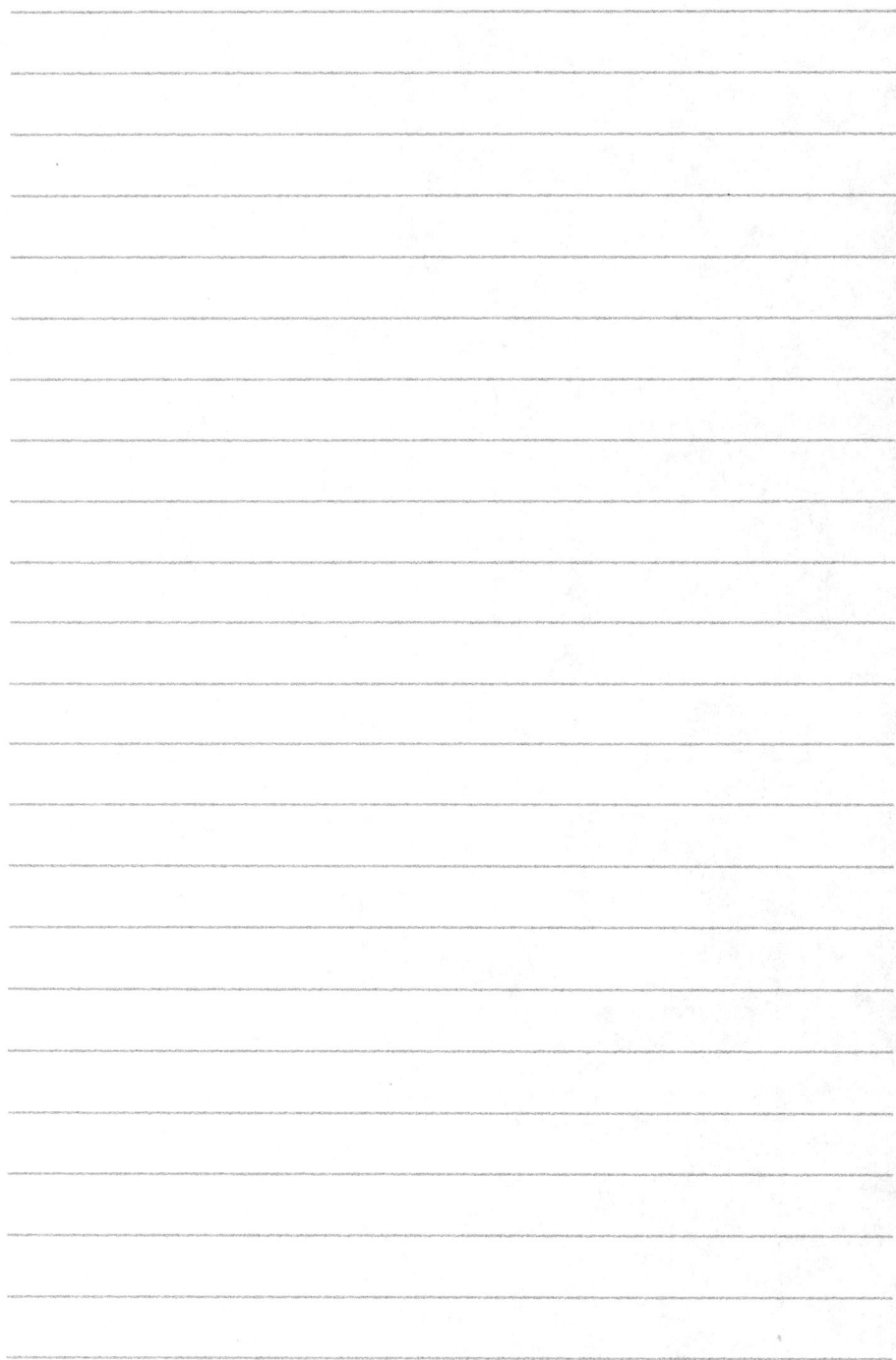

2 RECOVERING FROM INFIDELITY

This first exercise focusses on one of the most common areas for which couples and individuals seek counselling. Whether you are the betrayed person or the betrayer, you'll find resources here to help you process and heal from the trauma of such an event and find the meaning behind what has happened.

If your relationship hasn't experienced infidelity, express gratitude and simply move on to the next section of this workbook.

2.1 MEASURE THE SEVERITY OF BETRAYAL

Is it possible for a relationship to recover from infidelity? In short, yes. But in my experience, the severity of betrayal has much to do with whether the relationship can truly recover. That's not to say that if you have a severe case your relationship won't survive, but the time required and the amount of dedicated therapy you would need to commit to is greater as you move up the scale of severity.

If you are wrestling with infidelity—past or present—you're bound to be feeling raw. The following exercise can act as an impact assessment to help you gauge the severity of your situation. Recognize that the degree of intimacy, for example, is highly subjective and might be assumed. Sometimes emotional intimacy can trump physical intimacy and vice versa. This is why I recommend each of you complete this exercise separately to gauge your perception of the severity of betrayal—you are unlikely to share exactly the same perception in each case. In the space below each point, make any notes and rate the severity of each point for yourself: 0 being not at all severe and 3 being the most severe.

12 FACTORS OF SEVERITY OF BETRAYAL

1. Whether the affair was a one-off or long-term liaison.

2. Whether the other person/people were known to the betrayed person.

3. The degree of intimacy that was shared with the other person.

4. Whether the betrayer had/has feelings for the other person.

5. Whether the betrayal was spontaneous or premeditated and planned.

6. The timing of the affair in terms of the circumstances and hardships in the couple's life at the time, e.g., pregnancy, financial pressures, new baby, illness, depression, conflict, emotional and physical distance, grief.

7. The context for the affair: a colleague at work, online dating sites, live porn, trips away from home, a brothel, in one's home, and so on.

8. Whether this was the first time or a repeat betrayal.

9. How much the betrayed person was put at risk by the betrayer in terms of their welfare, privacy, protection, and dignity.

10. The degree and frequency of lies during the affair.

(0 1 2 3) _____

11. The degree and frequency of lies after the affair was discovered.

(0 1 2 3) _____

12. Who else knew about the affair/s.

(0 1 2 3) _____

2.2 RECOVERY STEPS FOR THE BETRAYED PERSON AND THE BETRAYER

Now that you are clearer about the severity of betrayal that you're wrestling with, take your time as you work through the process below.

- Choose the section that applies to you as either the betrayed person or the betrayer.
- Use the journaling page provided to note thoughts and feelings that come up for you.
- Tick each step when you have completed it.
- When the time feels right for you and your partner, sit down together and talk through each of the points.

2.2.1 THE RECOVERY PROCESS: FOR THE BETRAYER

1. Take responsibility. Come clean with your partner about *all* your betraying acts. If you engage in further deceptions, you'll sabotage your chances of rekindling trust and respect.
2. Identify the feelings your partner is internalising and what they believe your actions mean. Do the same for yourself.
3. Empathise with your partner's pain. Show genuine remorse and vulnerability.
4. Understand and have patience for your partner's anger, rage, contempt, and hold the space for them to vent.
5. Understand the cost to your partner's self-esteem, sense of safety, and self-worth. Do the same for yourself.

6. Answer your partner's questions again and again, but sense when the time for going over the same painful details is over. In *Choices*, remember Leigh's revelation in chapter 4, and recognise when it's time to call out your partner (gently) if you sense they've become attached to the trauma of what you did, sabotaging their ability to heal. Calling time on your partner's questioning, though, is likely to be months rather than weeks away.
7. Proactively seek to find out how your partner is doing and be open to talking with them about it.
8. Share your understanding of what motivated you to stray from the relationship. How did you feel about yourself, and what were the payoffs for you when you were cheating? This is a very important question, and the answer will help your partner process how you could have made the choice to look elsewhere.
9. Be transparent with your communication devices. Do not hide anything.
10. Keep your word on the smallest details going forward. Don't over-promise and under-deliver.
11. Seek individual counselling and start the process of self-forgiveness. Guilt is self-punishing and gets you nowhere in the long run.
12. Develop your personal code of honour, one that you will hold *yourself* to, and share your pledge with your partner.
13. If you know you want to restore your relationship, show your partner—in ways that matter to them—that they are wanted.

2.2.2 THE RECOVERY PROCESS: FOR THE PERSON BETRAYED

1. Share your feelings with your partner and what you believe their actions mean—for you, for them, and for the relationship.
2. Be explicit and realistic about what you need in order to work through the trauma. (Perhaps you need time apart to reflect and heal).
3. Watch out for misery attracting misery. Manage your thoughts and avoid spiralling into irrational thinking and behaviour which could be a convenient distraction from doing the work that's needed.
4. Give yourself time to find your truth. Try not to make knee-jerk decisions from a place of fear, hurt, and pride.
5. Avoid making the affair about the other person your partner cheated on you with. Focus on what is within your control, e.g., you, your reactions, your relationship, and the relative strengths, merits, weaknesses, and voids.
6. Allow your partner time to process their shame. It takes time for defensiveness to give way to self-awareness so that the vulnerability of true remorse can be experienced and shown.
7. Have boundaries on your own need for control. Endless sleuthing and interrogating is fear-based and seldom helpful. Your partner is far more likely to step towards you with their truth when you let go of control.
8. Consider your negating patterns in relationships and the work that's required to raise your self-esteem.
9. Self-soothe with positive self-talk and enabling behaviour.
10. Take responsibility for your own denial and absence (be it mental, emotional, or physical) from the relationship.
11. Don't take responsibility for your partner's behaviour. Regardless of whatever errors you've made, you're not responsible for your partner's choices, feelings, or behaviour, and vice versa.
12. Seek the key to get out of your stuckness. There comes a time when you choose to get over it or you risk having an affair with the affair.

2.2.3 FIND MEANING THROUGH THIS TRAUMA

- Consider the pillars of trust, hope, respect, and love that might still exist in the wake of the betrayal. If there is reasonable evidence that just one of these pillars remains standing, lean on that pillar while you work to repair the pillars that have been pillaged.
- Commit to counselling and use the safe place to set boundaries and navigate the unspeakable.
- Remember the whole person in your partner, not just the behaviour that led to this.
- Limit how you navigate this trauma. Avoid adding fuel to the flame by piling on unfinished business and dragging up the dirt.
- Keep your circles of privacy small, and only engage with third parties who can be discreet, objective, supportive, and helpful. Remember: this is your relationship. Don't feel pressured by other people and their agendas.
- Share your ideas and wants for mending/developing a safety net of trust in the relationship.

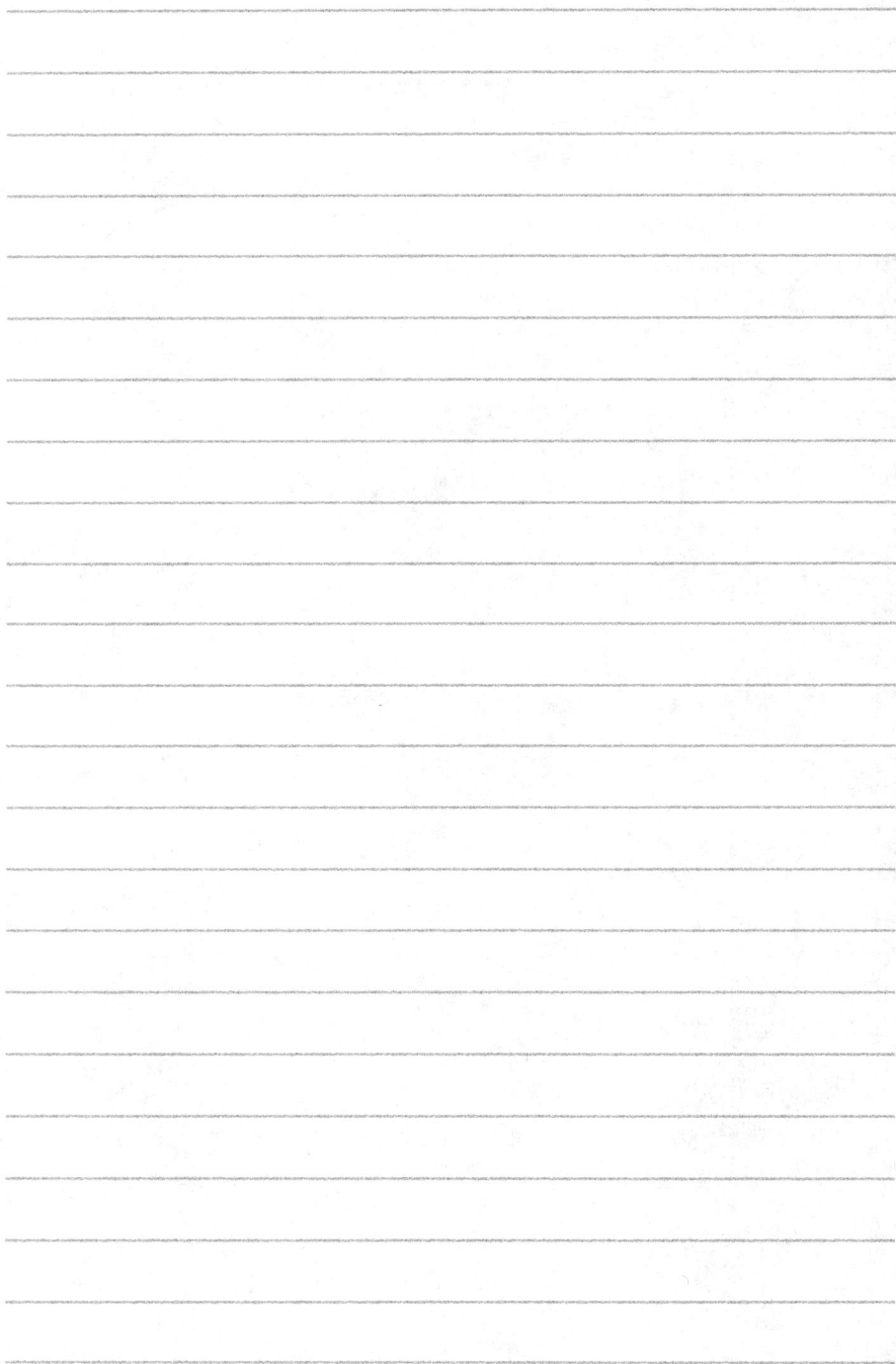

3 WANTS AND EXPECTATIONS

Knowing what you want is the first step to a fulfilled life. For more on this concept, refer back to chapter 8, "Choose Truth," in *Choices*. It's important to be clear about what you expect from yourself in a relationship, from the relationship itself, and from your partner, and to be proactive in sharing your expectations with them.

Taking this step will ensure both parties are in the know about what they're signing up for and united in what they hope to achieve together. You'll also have mutual understanding as to what's in each other's mind's eye early on in the relationship—before you find the relationship is not turning out as hoped. Giving each other the head's up on your expectations gives you the chance to commit and contract in agreement or revise and compromise where there's disparity.

3.1 EXPECTATIONS VS. EXPERIENCE – DISCUSSION POINTS

I have yet to meet a client who is not in some way grieving the gap between what they want and what they have.

Choosing to enter into or stay in a relationship with neither a compass nor a rudder is sure to steer you straight into the doldrums, where lack of fulfilment, frustration, and boredom reside. Relationships need a true north, a heading that incorporates the wants, dreams, and intentions of both personalities, providing a pulling force packed with direction and purpose.

This exercise will help you clarify what you expect of yourself as well as what you expect of your relationship.

You and your partner can each complete this journaling exercise separately and then come together to review and discuss your answers.

What's lacking, and what's working?

_____

_____

_____

_____

Are you both proactive and pitching up, or is one putting in more effort?

_____

_____

_____

_____

Do you each have the freedom to be yourselves?

_____

_____

_____

_____

What have you recently learnt about your partner?

_____

_____

_____

_____

What challenges you about each other currently?

Do you *want* to be together, or do you feel you *have* to be together?

What do you need to forgive and let go of?

Do you regard yourself as growing in the relationship? If not, what's needed?

Are there any relationships you envy? What qualities evident in those relationships can be incorporated into your own?

If you have previously set intentions together for the relationship, are they still relevant? Do you still have consensus, or do you need a fresh start?

3.2 THIS IS WHAT I WANT

Sit down with your partner to apply yourselves to this exercise, and my tip is to head for *real*, not *surreal*, outcomes. Realistic expectations are achievable and sustainable, whereas surreal notions often come from an idyllic, romanticised view of how a relationship should be. When your relationship starts to settle into its everyday pattern, a surrealistic outlook will have you regarding your relationship as mediocre or underwhelming when in fact it may well be solid and substantial. Know that whatever you want your relationship to be, you must be willing to gear and steer it in that direction yourself.

3.2.1 IDENTIFY

Identify your wants and expectations by reminding yourself of your core values. Examples of positive values that clients have identified as forming the basis of their wants include:
- honesty and transparency
- affection and attentiveness

- engagement and communication
- fallibility and vulnerability
- forgiveness and mercy
- equality and partnership
- loyalty and respect
- freedom and growth

Having reflected on the above, list your core values below.

1. _____

2. _____

3. _____

4. _____

5. _____

6. _____

7. _____

8. _____

9. _____

10. _____

11. _____

12. _____

3.2.2 REVIEW

With your core values to ground you, review all aspects of your desired relationship and the associated expectations. Ponder the aspects that keep the relationship colourful and energised, that keep it functioning well, the responsibilities that keep it accountable, and the freedoms that enable you to grow and be yourself. Ask yourself what fulfils you, from head to heart to behaviour. Now go ahead and list at least thirty expectations you have of a relationship—don't hold back!

Once you have your list of thirty expectations, rate the importance of each item on your list of expectations from 0–5 using the space alongside your listing, which will help you distinguish the fundamental from the superficial.

Expectation	Rating
1	
2	
3	
4	
5	
6	
7	
8	
9	
10	
11	
12	
13	
14	

Expectation	Rating
15	
16	
17	
18	
19	
20	
21	
22	
23	
24	
25	
26	
27	
28	
29	
30	

3.2.3 REFLECT

Reflect on your list and consider your own ability to give yourself what you are expecting your partner to give to you. Pay particular attention to the expectations that are critically important to you but which you are poor at giving yourself.

3.2.4 SHARE

Share your insights with your partner. Listen to understand and ensure that you don't make assumptions and get tripped up in semantics. For example, if your partner wants transparency in the relationship, what does that mean for them? What would it look like as behaviour?

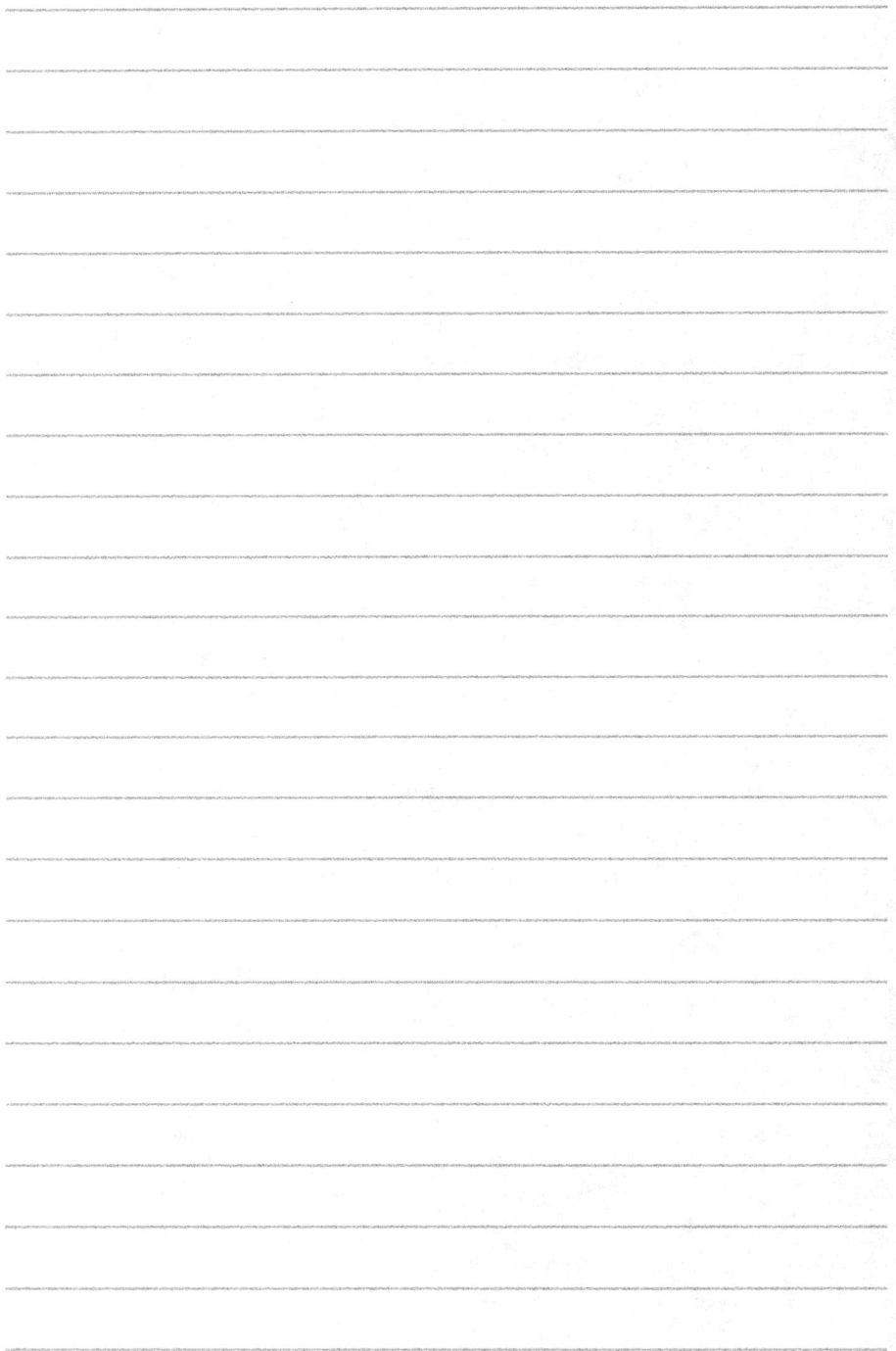

4 CHOOSE TO TRUST YOUR VOICE: THOUGHT-CODING FOR RELATIONSHIPS

What you think about and say to yourself, you are likely to manifest. And your thoughts determine the emotions that are triggered and, ultimately, your behaviour comes about as a result of those thoughts and feelings.

This is easy to spell out, but not easy to unwind. That's because our thoughts are running on unconscious programmes that started before we could talk. (I write in more detail about this programming in chapter 9, "Choose Trust," in *Choices*.)

If we don't find a way to manage the ways in which we think and access the quality and value of what we think about, these thought programmes have a way of setting us up for defeat. Therefore, cleaning the hallways of your mind and building new thought programmes and pathways is essential if you want to override your hardwiring and address the harmful attachment patterns which may be sabotaging your chances of relationship success. It's pointless wishing for a happy marriage with the script of "I'm always overlooked; I am unimportant; and I am undesirable" running through your internal headset.

Unbundle the irrelevant, unhelpful, and expired cognitions that tag along in your shadow, and trade in that jaded headset for a script that talks to your true, inimitable, and worthy self. See how life rises up to prove that script right.

Here's an exercise I use extensively with my clients and that my family continues to use to this day. Become the author of your own narrative and develop your own cheerleading thought companion.

4.1 RESTRAINTS

Reflect on the disabling events, opinions, people, patterns, beliefs, feelings, and assumptions that are restraining you from being your best self at present. List and describe those in the left-hand column of the table below.

4.2 BENEFITS

For each of the restraints you've identified, write down the benefits or pay-offs, i.e. how that restraint *serves* you. For example: If you believe that being overweight is holding you back, you might also recognise that there are benefits to you being overweight. For instance, perhaps the weight feels like a protective layer against being hurt, and maybe it gives you an excuse to stay at home to avoid rejection or failure.

You might feel inclined to say there are no benefits to having restraints, but challenge yourself...the benefits are there, especially if that restraint allows you to avoid some discomfort. Benefits often go undetected and can be very sneaky.

What's holding me back?	The benefits of my restraints …

What's holding me back?	The benefits of my restraints …

4.3 FUTURE YOU

Imagine that you have the ability to see into the future. You catch a preview of yourself in a relationship three months from now. In this picture, you are no longer restrained and are your most magnificent best. In that new landscape, ponder who you are with, where you are, and what has changed about you/the context. Now, write down the myriad desired feelings you imagine you would have if you were your magnificent best.

MY DESIRED FEELINGS – THREE MONTHS FROM NOW

4.4 DESIGN WHO YOU ARE

Design your "I Am" statements. Refer to the feelings you identified in 3.3 above and write your script, one line at a time. Do this by identifying three feelings at a time that work well together, starting with the words "I am." For example, "I am courageous, determined, and free to be me." For best results and to avoid fatigue, write a maximum of ten sentences with a maximum of three feelings/values in each sentence. Write them so they flow easily when spoken out loud.

MY THOUGHT-CODE

I am…

4.5 YOUR NEW THOUGHTS APP

"Download" your Thoughts App. Your Thoughts App will take at least one month to download. To download it, read your text for fifteen minutes *daily*—out loud, quickly, and without concentrating on what the words mean. (Why fifteen minutes? This is a proven treatment plan called Accelerated Behavioural Cognitive Therapy, and fifteen minutes is required if the change is to be achieved.) As a back-up, you can record yourself doing this exercise as instructed above and if you don't get around to doing your lines in person, you can simply listen to your recording for fifteen minutes. But don't make a habit of this, just use it when absolutely necessary as it's better than missing a day.

If you miss one day, you need to double up the next day, and if you miss two consecutive days, you need to start the programme again. After four weeks of this daily recitation, you can write a new script which might tackle the way you think in more detail e.g., "I finish what I start; I speak to crowds with confidence; and I am a healthy weight of sixty kilograms."

Check out this script by way of example.

1. I pursue excellence; I rescue myself and take responsibility for my life.
2. I leave the past behind; I trust myself to take risks; I am courageous.
3. I am worthy, lovable, and open-hearted.
4. I am present, attentive, and empathetic.
5. I attract like-minded people; I am energised and inspired.
6. I respect myself and others; I am enthusiastic and curious.
7. I like who I am; I accept who I am; I am healed.
8. I am whole, content, and happy.

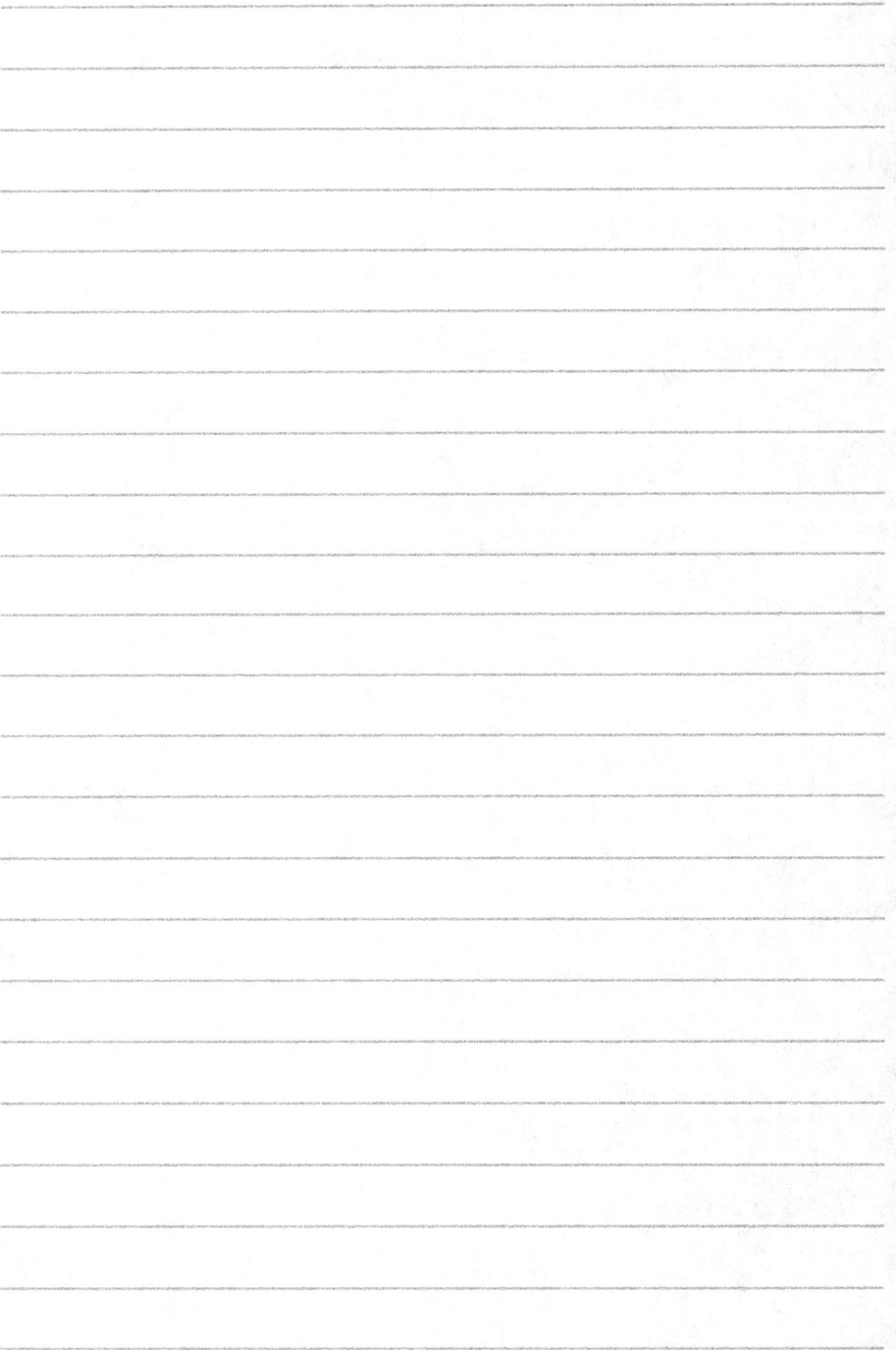

5 CHOOSE RESPECT

Respect is a master choice and one you will find detailed in chapter 10, "Choose Respect," of *Choices*.

Respect is both an attitude and an emotion. We respect people who personify qualities we ourselves possess, and we respect those who embody qualities to which we aspire. A good barometer on how your relationship is doing is to assess if your self-respect and self-esteem feel uplifted. If they don't, there's a big red flag that you need to take responsibility for some changes because you might be negotiating away critical parts of yourself.

Turning your regard for yourself from one of blame and judgment to acceptance and respect will be a game changer. Here follows a quick audit to help you raise your awareness as to how you value and demonstrate respect towards yourself and to nudge you towards walking your talk that is respectful towards yourself—before expecting others to respect you.

5.1 THE SELF-RESPECT AUDIT AND DISCUSSION TOPIC

Sit down as a couple and, using these prompts, ask for feedback from each other and encourage yourself to be feedback fit.

DO YOU...

Limit your own negative behaviour?

_____

_____

_____

Place limits on something or someone that is disabling for you?

Stand up for yourself when you feel wronged?

Stand up for yourself—your ideas, opinions, and dreams?

Put yourself first?

Honour and share your feelings?

Honour, share, and work towards having your *wants* met?

Guard your self-esteem?

Soothe and forgive yourself when you fail and appreciate growth from such events?

_____

_____

_____

_____

_____

Allow yourself the freedom to fail?

_____

_____

_____

_____

_____

Seek partners and friends who match your degree of self-respect?

_____

_____

_____

_____

_____

Take care of yourself?

_____

_____

_____

Take time to develop yourself, to grow mentally, emotionally, physically, and spiritually?

Ensure that you are reliable?

Keep true to yourself aligning your thoughts, feelings, and behaviours?

Correct yourself and take responsibility when you let yourself and others down?

Honour your inner "no's" by not going with the tide or by saying "yes" just to please?

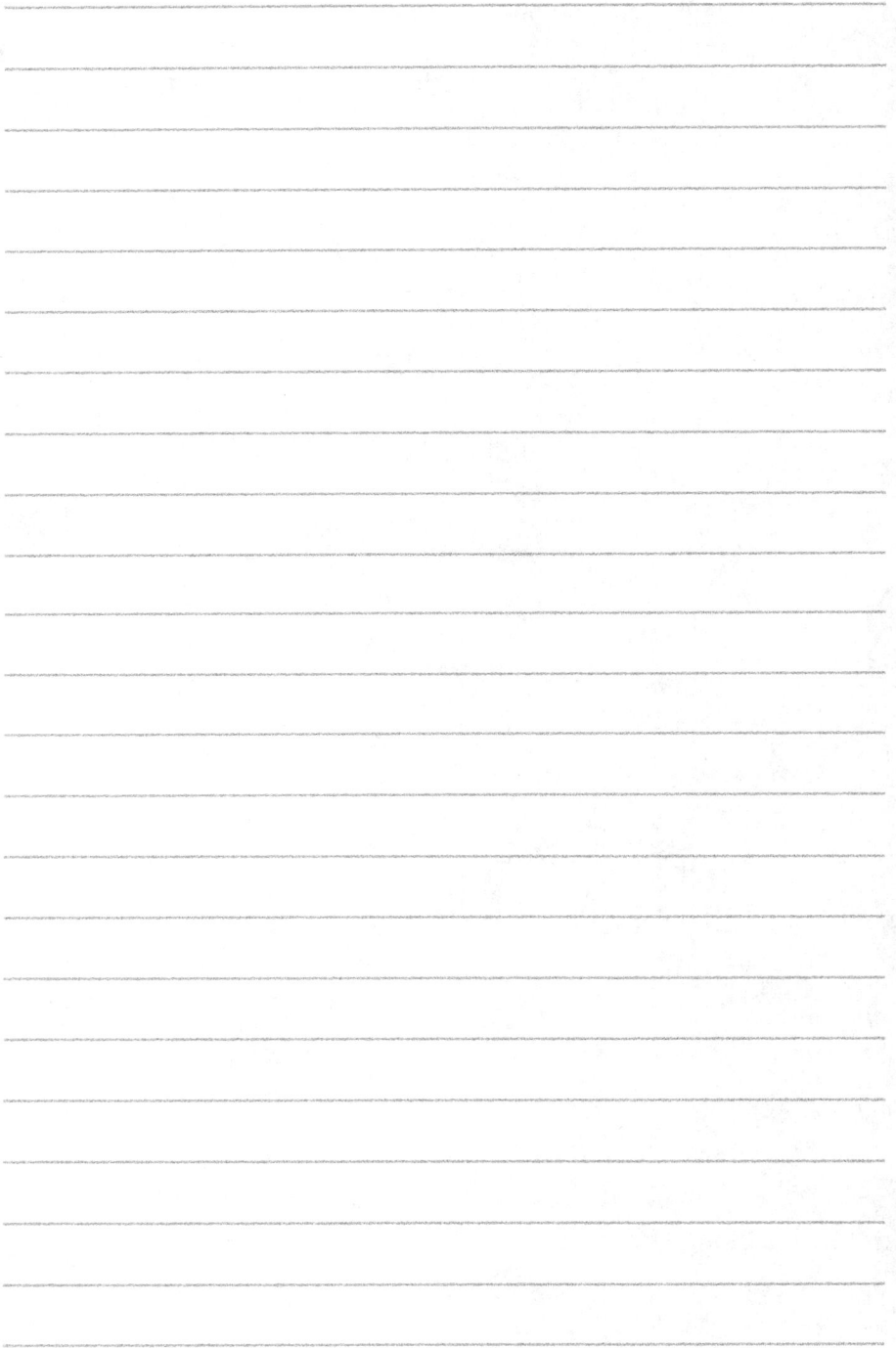

6 CHOOSE TENDERNESS AND FORGIVENESS

Bitterness and resentment cannot coexist with tenderness and forgiveness.

It takes a self-aware person to recognize that they need—and want—to let go and forgive someone. True forgiveness requires humility, empathy, and a whole lot of adulting. If you've realized that you are holding onto a heap of unforgiveness towards your partner or key people in your life, re-read chapter 11, "Choose Tenderness," in *Choices* to remind yourself that you can choose to stop the victimhood of unforgiveness in its tracks.

Forgiveness is another master choice and the gateway to reclaiming your own tenderness given that it allows you to take responsibility for the resentment that you hold towards others and yourself. Forgiveness is one of the hardest qualities to master but worth the effort as it's the antidote to blame and judgment. It keeps you in your truth and reminds you that we're human and we all err.

6.1 TEN STEPS TO FORGIVENESS

It is not easy to reach a state of forgiveness, especially if the transgressions have been deeply hurtful or plentiful. The following ten steps will help you release the self-punishment of withholding forgiveness and regain lost tenderness.

Step 1 Identify all the feelings you experienced in relation to the event.

Step 2 Identify what you understood your partner's behaviour said about you personally (this is the meaning you derive from it).

Step 3 Identify whether any part of you agreed with the meaning you took out of this event.

_____

_____

_____

_____

_____

_____

_____

_____

_____

Step 4 Question whether you played any part in provoking this event and review how you handled the event when it happened.

_____

_____

_____

_____

_____

_____

_____

_____

Step 5 Review whether you have communicated the impact on you and your relationship by sharing your feelings and the meaning you took away from it.

_____

_____

_____

_____

_____

_____

_____

_____

Step 6 Consider your partner's level of remorse or attempt at taking responsibility.

_____

_____

_____

_____

_____

_____

_____

Step 7 Acknowledge the severity of this event and how attached you feel to not forgiving that it happened.

Step 8 Imagine how you would feel emotionally, mentally, physically, and spiritually, if you were able to let this event go.

Step 9 Choose to forgive your partner and yourself (where applicable) and allow tenderness to soothe the feelings in you that have been over-looked and neglected.

Step 10 Remind yourself that forgiveness is a process and for it to take effect, equal amounts of tenderness and patience towards yourself are required.

Here are some additional suggestions to be mindful of as you work to forgive.

- Remind yourself that your partner is bigger than their behaviour, and avoid limiting them to a stereotype he/she (or you) can't escape.
- Forgiveness requires that you reignite your tenderness to empathise with your partner's fallibility. Confess to yourself whether the theme of their behaviour is something that you have experienced or yourself done before, e.g., dishonesty, rebellion, disrespect, sleuthing, double-standards, neglect, etc.
- Reflect on the context of your partner's life at the time of the event and see if it informs what happened.
- Isolate your own reactions to the event, i.e., what did it hook in you?
- Notice what you believe your partner has not yet learnt to do.
- Try to imagine your partner's opinion of themselves with regards to the event.

6.2 WRITE A FORGIVENESS LETTER

Plan for this exercise by finding a space that is pleasant and private, where you will be undisturbed. Give yourself at least an hour to work through the questions. If you are working with your partner and wish to forgive them in this exercise, tear out the page when you have completed it, read it to them, and hand it to them so they can reflect on it in their own time.

Once in your quiet place, recall the event/s and person you want to forgive. Involve your senses—take in what you can recall, what you saw, smelled, heard, tasted, and felt. Immerse yourself in the memory whilst re-assuring yourself that you are safe and in control of the narrative.

As you recall the event, notice your own reactions such as pain, fear, nausea, repulsion, anxiety, hopelessness, helplessness, bitterness, and so on. Give permission for these feelings to exist in this moment and, by so doing, validate them.

Now notice your thoughts towards this event and person—notice your personal reality about what happened. Although the other person might remember it differently, the version you have is the one you need to forgive.

And on a cautionary note, don't go in with an agenda that can't be met. The person who receives your letter might not appreciate your forgiveness and might get defensive and refute your version of what happened. Remember your purpose. You are doing this to let go, not hold on. The other person might not be where you are and let that be ok.

Now read this sample letter which offers some details that you might find relevant. Using your own words, take a deep breathe, pick up your pen, and begin to write:

Date _____

Dear _____

Please accept this letter which is about me forgiving and letting go. Writing this has not been easy, but it is necessary.

I have realized that I need to forgive you for

_____

_____

_____

_____

When this/these events happened, I felt

_____

_____

_____

_____

This event/s/your behaviour had me believing

_____

_____

_____

_____

I acknowledge that I played a role in these events by

_____

_____

_____

_____

And I accept responsibility for my part.

I have reflected on your level of remorse (not just shows of guilt) and your attempts at taking responsibility for what happened. I acknowledge that you have

_____

_____

_____

_____

But I also recognise that you haven't

_____

_____

_____

_____

And I have needed to accept that.

I've also considered that certain circumstances may have contributed towards your behaviour, such as

_____

_____

_____

_____

_____

I recognise that I have been somewhat / significantly / extremely attached to the trauma of this event/s and to not letting go or forgiving what happened.

However, when I consider myself being freed of my unforgiveness and acknowledge how I would feel emotionally, mentally, physically, and spiritually, I then realise that I am punishing myself by not forgiving you.

I am choosing to let go of unforgiveness, and I am choosing to forgive you. By so doing, I am not in any way condoning your behaviour/ what happened. But I am acknowledging that you are fallible and worthy of forgiveness, and that I am capable of un-attaching myself from the grip of this memory/ memories.

Finally, I understand that forgiveness is a process and that I have taken the first step in what might take a little / some time / a long time to accomplish.

Thank you for reading this. I don't need a response / I would appreciate your response.

Kind regards,

Congratulate yourself for taking this bold and defining step. You might choose to post this letter, deliver it by hand, read it to the person or proxy, or simply let the letter be a testament to your forgiveness without the person ever knowing you wrote it. (The latter is commonplace when the person you need to forgive has passed away).

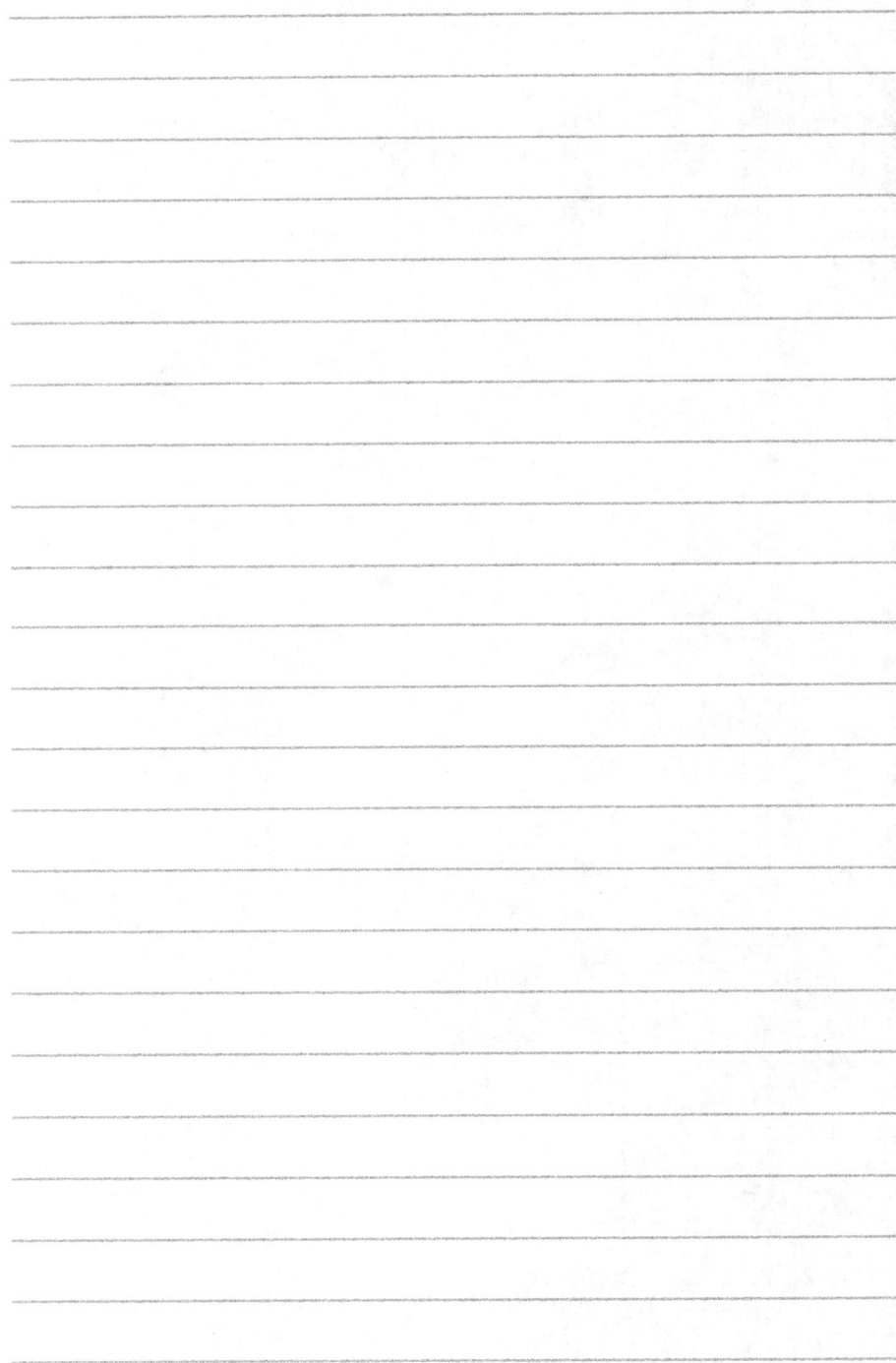

7 CHOOSE LISTENING

The major reason relationships fail is due to poor communication—not due to infidelity, as is widely assumed. Almost every couple I've met that attends counselling lists communication as a weakness, and their aim is to master the skill.

Communication is a two-way street: there's the delivery and the receipt. To choose to listen well requires that we also learn to share well.

Take a look at these discussion points, and write your thoughts or comments to yourself. Remember to allow yourself the freedom to fail, and don't take yourself too seriously. Have fun!

7.1 SHARING TO BE HEARD

When you want to be heard, choose to be mindful and self-regulate your own approach and behaviour, using the following guidelines:

- Accept that your feelings are legitimate and you have a right to be heard.
- Accept that your feelings are your own, and while they may arise in response to someone else's behaviour, they are not the responsibility of that person.
- Stay on topic and within the bounds of the current relationship.
- Avoid shouting at your listener or covering your mouth, limiting your audibility.
- Maintain eye contact.
- Be patient with your listener when they interrupt you and attempt to reflect what you've said and remember that what they hear will be filtered by their own reality.
- Slow down, breathe deeply, and articulate clearly.

- If your listener interjects in defence or to correct you, stop them and remind them that you have not finished but that you do want to hear their response, once you're done.
- Allow yourself to show vulnerability.
- Stick to the time that you both agreed on to share your side of the story. A person can only listen effectively in short runs (about five to eight minutes, max) before they will need to respond.

7.2 RESPONSIVE LISTENING EXAMPLES

Responsive listening means responding to what you are witnessing in the present moment. It has the potential to create a magnetic energy where both parties feel connected and rooted in the now.

Reflecting how a conversation has you feeling while it is happening anchors you to the here and now, signals that you are not anywhere else but there in front of that person, and that you are paying attention to them completely. Responses that show you are present, receptive, and paying attention include:

- What a lovely thing to say. That makes me feel so valued! Thank you.
- Thank you for sharing your news with me. I feel excited along with you.
- Thank you for sharing something so intimate with me. I feel so trusted.
- Your eyes tell me you're disappointed about something...
- I'm confused. You are smiling right now, but that doesn't tie up with what you're saying...
- Your tone and energy seems low. Are you tired?
- Your speech is very rapid. I can tell you are stressed.

Discuss the above with your partner and add a few of your own sentences that you would like to practice saying in the future.

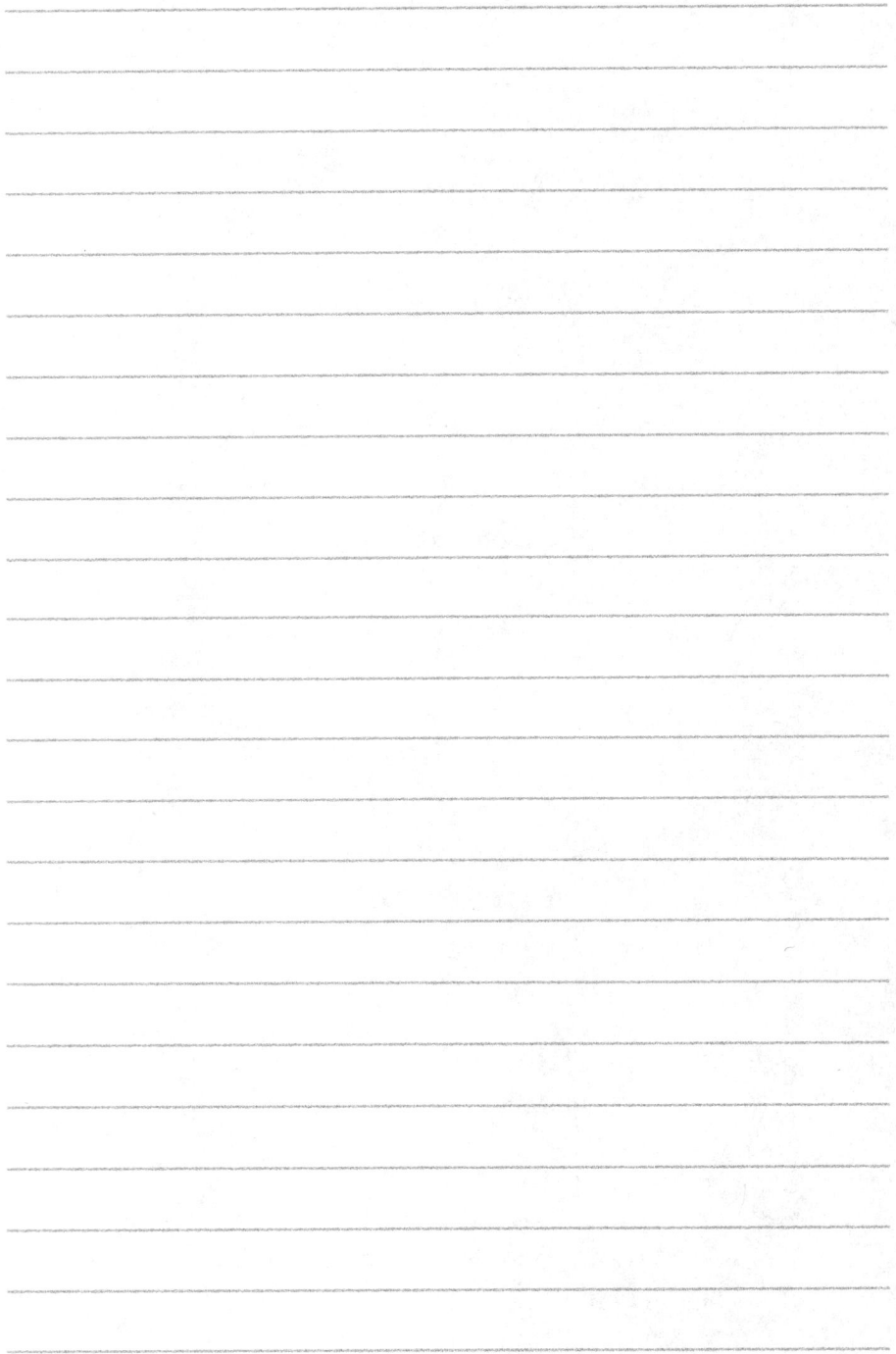

8 TOUGH CONVERSATIONS CHOOSE TO FIGHT FAIR

Managing conflict well is a skill we can all benefit from. It's probably one of the factors that had you reaching for *Choices* in the first place. Most couples begin to struggle with their relationships when fights become regular, go below the belt, and become more about winning and being right than about being heard and understood.

You can choose to fight fair. These are the key steps to become familiar with so you can graduate toward having difficult conversations that result in increased intimacy, connection, mutual respect, and understanding. You might not agree with the other person, but you should be clear about and accept their right to have their own view. Practice makes perfect as well as giving yourself the freedom to fail. Back your instincts on needing to prioritise this skill because if there is one thing that can save your relationship from an early crash, it's learning to fight fair. Refer to chapter 14, "Choose to Fight Fair," for more information on this subject.

8.1 PREPARE FOR A DISRUPTIVE CONVERSATION

Conscious and fair conflict requires that you are clear about your role in the conflict and where you stand—your hooks, triggers, and overall circumstances at that point in time.

Reflect on the relationship, the person with whom you have this conflict, and their importance and relevance in your life.

8.2 CHECK IN WITH YOURSELF

Imagine a best-case scenario and how you would like the relationship to be.

_____

_____

_____

_____

_____

_____

Come back to today and review the relationship, how you treat this person, and how they treat you.

_____

_____

_____

_____

_____

_____

Recognise what you are feeling in response to their behaviour and this relationship.

_____

_____

_____

_____

_____

_____

Acknowledge what you are resisting about them or yourself. For example, perhaps their arrogance antagonises your lack of confidence, or their helplessness prompts the discomfort you feel regarding areas of your life where you, too, are not in control.

_____

_____

_____

_____

What negative self-belief does this person confirm within you?

_____

_____

_____

_____

8.3 REFLECT ON THE OTHER PERSON

What meaning do you assume they are taking on about you, and what feelings are they experiencing in relation to you?

_____

_____

_____

_____

_____

Imagine what their initial expectations of the relationship or of you were.

Try to imagine what they find the hardest about their relationship with you. In other words, what's the one big thing they have to overcome or accept?

Ponder whether they are coming from a place of love for themselves or fear of what might happen. If it's fear, how are they attempting to control their fear?

8.4 REFLECT ON THE RELATIONSHIP

Identify what you have in common by way of meanings, feelings, wants, and hurdles.

_____

_____

_____

_____

_____

_____

What do each of you have in common by way of personality, values, and personal history?

_____

_____

_____

_____

_____

What is it about the other person you resist the most, and how does that same trait show up in you?

_____

_____

_____

_____

With these three exercises covered, you will have opened the door for your self-awareness to work in your favour. Hopefully your own truth-telling has connected you to being *real* as opposed to being in *control*.

General communication is an art but is reasonably easy to learn. Disruptive conversations, on the other hand, are tricky for most of us to navigate and require boundaries if we're to manage well.

8.5 ASSUME THE RIGHT ATTITUDE FOR A DISRUPTIVE CONVERSATION

The following inner boundaries give conversations, especially tough ones, the best chance of an outcome matching your intention.

Set your intention for the discussion.

\
\
\
\
\
\

Identify how your behaviour and communication approach is going to align with your intention.

\
\
\
\
\
\

- Drop any crutches that you might perceive as giving you an added advantage over the other person, e.g., alcohol, non-neutral places, top-dog language.
- Give up the need to be right.
- Give up the need to win.
- Give up the need to have the last say.
- Observe whether you are inclined to download and dump information on your listener and make a conscious choice to communicate well, to be heard and understood.
- Value communicating in a way that shares your thoughts, feelings, and wants, not just your opinions.
- Give up the need for your partner to mirror your views and accept that your partner has a different reality to yours. And don't take that personally! That's what makes them who they are.
- Accept that you are going to feel vulnerable and exposed and trust that you can soothe yourself through this process.
- Give up any attachments you might have to the outcome of the discussion. (Your initial intention should have more to do with your behaviour rather than the other person). Value the truth and integrity of representing your values. This one is tricky and reminds me of the saying: "What you value is what you'll have."

8.6 WHAT NOT TO DO WHEN MANAGING CONFLICT

Discuss the following "don'ts" with your partner and acknowledge whether you or your partner use these tactics. When you bring your partner's attention to their maneuvers, be careful not to get into blame mode but keep mindful that you are sharing what stops you from being able to listen with an open heart.

1. Don't bring in the cavalry (Your mom agrees with me on this....)

2. Don't drag up the dirt or load the gun with more than what's on the table at that moment. (This will overwhelm your listener and have them withdraw or become defensive).

3. Don't cross-question and pressure your partner into getting their facts right—stay away from entering a battle for power. Listen to understand their way of seeing the story. Be curious about their reality, even if you can see they're mistaken and their version differs from yours. (By validating their version first, you will open the door for you giving your version, wherein they might see and take responsibility for their own mistakes).

4. Don't name-call or use stereotypes that are likely to provoke your partner. ("You are such a control freak." "You are such a victim." etc.)

5. Don't roll your eyes, avoid eye contact, or turn your body away from your partner.

6. Don't use absolutes like "you always…" or "you never…" This provokes defensiveness.

7. Don't threaten to leave or end the relationship because you are arguing. This is a flight response and strips away the safety net of the relationship, ensuring the next round of conflict is even harder.

8. Don't become a tyrant, abusive, or threatening towards your partner (a fight response). A raised voice is to be expected, but shouting, swearing, and invading your partner's space is off limits and bound to end in disaster.

In essence, steer clear from blame and judgment and stop making a victim out of you and your partner.

8.7 TEN TIPS FOR THE CONSCIOUS CONVERSATION

Now that you're conscious about what not to do, pick a challenging subject that tends to bring you discomfort. Then read the following pointers from top to bottom and consider how these will help you and your partner prepare for the discussion.

Ensure that you know what you're going to say, and sit in front of your partner, sticking to the boundaries that you've agreed to.

1. Thank the person for coming and acknowledge what it might have taken (time, courage, open-mindedness) to get them there.
2. Use the person's name—often—it acknowledges them directly.
3. State what you hope to achieve from having the conversation with them.
4. Seek agreement on the boundaries to the meeting: how long you'll take, that you not interrupt each other, and if relevant, agree to what each of you regard as showstoppers, e.g., shouting, name calling, a patronizing tone, etc.
5. Raise common ground early in the conversation. It helps to hedge against the sense of being completely opposed to one another, e.g., "We are both competitive people..." or "We both know what it's like to be caught in the middle between two people we love," etc.
6. Adopt a philosophy of graciousness. Acknowledge admirable qualities in the person while addressing the aspects that you find destructive.
7. Use "I" more frequently than you use "you." Take more responsibility than you attribute blame.
8. Don't perceive a differing opinion as dislike for you and let your fears hook you into a power-play. Accept that you are different people with differing views.
9. Allow yourself to show your feelings as and when they occur. Revealed feelings build trust and invite reciprocation. When you reveal your feelings, people are more likely to recognise, respect, and show more responsibility towards you.
10. Encourage your partner to interrupt you only when they need to clarify what they heard you say. This ensures reflective listening and will serve to validate and recognise both your feelings and your reasoning.

NOTES

....

....

....

_____

_____

_____

_____

_____

_____

_____

_____

8.7.1 THE SPEAKER'S CONVERSATION FLOW

Use this template to prepare your conversation.

"I've been thinking..." (Share your thoughts about the topic and the facts related to it. This is head talk.)

_____

_____

_____

_____

_____

_____

_____

_____

_____

_____

"And I've been feeling..." (Share the emotions that these issues bring up for you and try to offer up the depth or severity of that emotion, e.g., very vulnerable, somewhat overlooked, extremely angry. This is heart talk.)

"And what I really want is ..." (Share the way forward and be concise, e.g., for you to notice me when I come home. This is behaviour talk and represents you taking responsibility for what you want as an outcome.)

Incorporating head, heart, and behaviour will have you pitching up with integrity and offering a composite, graspable message—even if it's challenging—that gives you a good chance of being heard and understood by your partner.

8.7.2 THE LISTENER'S CONVERSATION FLOW

If you're the listener, interrupt your partner only to reflect what they feel due to the reasons *they* have shared. Don't ask questions or redirect the speaker towards your agenda. Trust that you are going to get a chance to respond when your partner is finished speaking. Your reflective listening method should follow this flow:

"Let me reflect what I have heard so far. I'm hearing that you feel..." (sad/mad/overlooked/deeply worried/etc. Make sure you are reflecting what you've picked up they might be feeling. Some speakers will not say what they feel, but they will act it out. You can misread what they're feeling, and that's ok because your attempt will still be better than not connecting with their feelings at all and getting the feeling wrong will nudge them to share the correct feeling.)

"Because ..." ("I don't greet you when I get home at night and I place so much importance on work"—reframe and share the reasons they gave you.)

"Is that right? Please go on..." (Encourage them to elaborate on their thread and reflect again and again until they feel completely heard. By the time they have exhausted the topic and you've reflected to the end, you will have arrived at a theme as to what is happening for your listener. The whole conversation, if you listen carefully, will reveal the speaker's underlying vulnerability and may arrive at a truth—like "If I am really honest, I am scared of losing you"—that will have you feeling so much closer to the person, and what started as conflict can result in great bonding and empathy.)

Even if the conversation does not go as you hoped, value the fact that you were proactive, that you gave your best effort. Commit to showing continued support to your own intentions for that relationship. Remember that trust in conversing around conflict takes time to build. If we are to get beyond the belief that conflict always ends in damage or injury, we need to aim for consistent, responsible behaviour.

8.8 TIPS TO KEEP CALM IN CONFLICT

Yep, we've all over-reacted and said hurtful things we later regret, because when our amygdala determines that we're not safe, our adrenaline and cortisol levels spike, shoving us into reactionary mode. Closed, single-mindedness that blocks out reason is the result—and invariably prevents the ability to use the above skills. This is the state that has my clients asking if these skills can ever really work in real life. Will they ever manage conflict well? Not without self intervention.

Limbic firing first needs quelling. You need time, space, breath work, and self-soothing to compose yourself before you can pass the ball up to the prefrontal cortex, which will bring you back to rational reasoning. Once your thinking comes from this part of your brain and you're in control of your emotions, you can return to the matter, take responsibility, and have an adult-to-adult round of effective conflict.

The Senses: Bring yourself into the present moment through your senses. Notice what you are feeling, smelling, seeing, hearing, and touching. Become aware of the floor/chair/bed upon which you are grounded.

Triggers: Notice what is triggering you. Become aware of these triggers and see them as red flags needing special navigation in future.

Breath: Breathe purposefully. Try the yogic pranayama technique whereby you sit comfortably and quietly and exhale through your mouth, letting all the stale air out. Then inhale through your nose only for the count of four. Then hold your breath for the count of seven. Then open your mouth releasing the air audibly through your mouth for the count of eight. Repeat this sequence for eight rounds.

Cognitions: Use one sentence from your Thought-Coding (exercise 3) that calms you. For example, "I am safe, calm under pressure, and make good decisions." Repeat your calming sentence fifty times.

8.9 CREATIVE CONVERSATIONS – UPDATING AND KEEPING IN SYNC

To stay current with your partner, to have the confidence to say that you truly know where they and the relationship are at today, and how it differs from yesterday, you must stay curious about what makes the other person tick and stay tuned in to one another's growth or regression.

If you're planning a date night and don't want to fall into the same rut of talking about the same draining topics—or perhaps hardly talking at all—test drive the following exercise for conversation prompts that are meaningful, energizing, and connecting. These topics are gate-openers to intimate and interesting updates on where the other person is and help you to gauge how the relationship is doing.

To prepare for this exercise, I suggest you both agree on the assumptions you'd like to talk about, choosing from the list below. Then take some time to list your answers (which are based on your assumption of your partner) without sharing until you've finished all your answers and are ready to talk. Then, take it in turns to respond to the selected prompts.

Chat to your partner about having more creative conversations. Mostly you'll want to speak spontaneously, but to see how your curiosity can be aroused when the topic is right, take a stab at these conversation prompts and note your answers in the space provided. Then give these topics a go at the dinner table or when you take your mate on a date.

I believe you are most motivated by...

I think your most important values right now are...

I think your prime expectation of yourself right now is...

I think your ideal holiday would be...

I think you still need to let go of/forgive yourself for...

_____

_____

_____

_____

If our house was burning down and everyone was safe but you had time to save one thing, I think you'd save...

_____

_____

_____

_____

The dream you still hold onto is...

_____

_____

_____

_____

The thought that most scares you is...

_____

_____

_____

_____

The feelings you experience often but least want are...

_____

_____

_____

_____

_____

The biggest area of disappointment for you in our relationship is...

_____

_____

_____

_____

_____

The greatest achievement for you in our relationship is...

_____

_____

_____

_____

_____

If there was one thing you could change about yourself, it would be...

_____

_____

_____

_____

If there was one thing you could change about me, it would be...

What you want more of in our relationship is...

What you want less of in our relationship is...

I think you feel needed when I...

I think you feel wanted when I...

_____

_____

_____

_____

When it comes to us, you think you have to...

_____

_____

_____

_____

When it comes to us, the things you don't have to do but want to do are...

_____

_____

_____

_____

What you need more of in your life is...

_____

_____

_____

_____

If you only had one word to describe what you hope the next five years will be remembered for, I think it would be...

Now you have some topics that will have you discovering each other all over again. Instead of being a rather dull couple with nothing to say, you'll be one of those couples who still have so much to discover about one another.

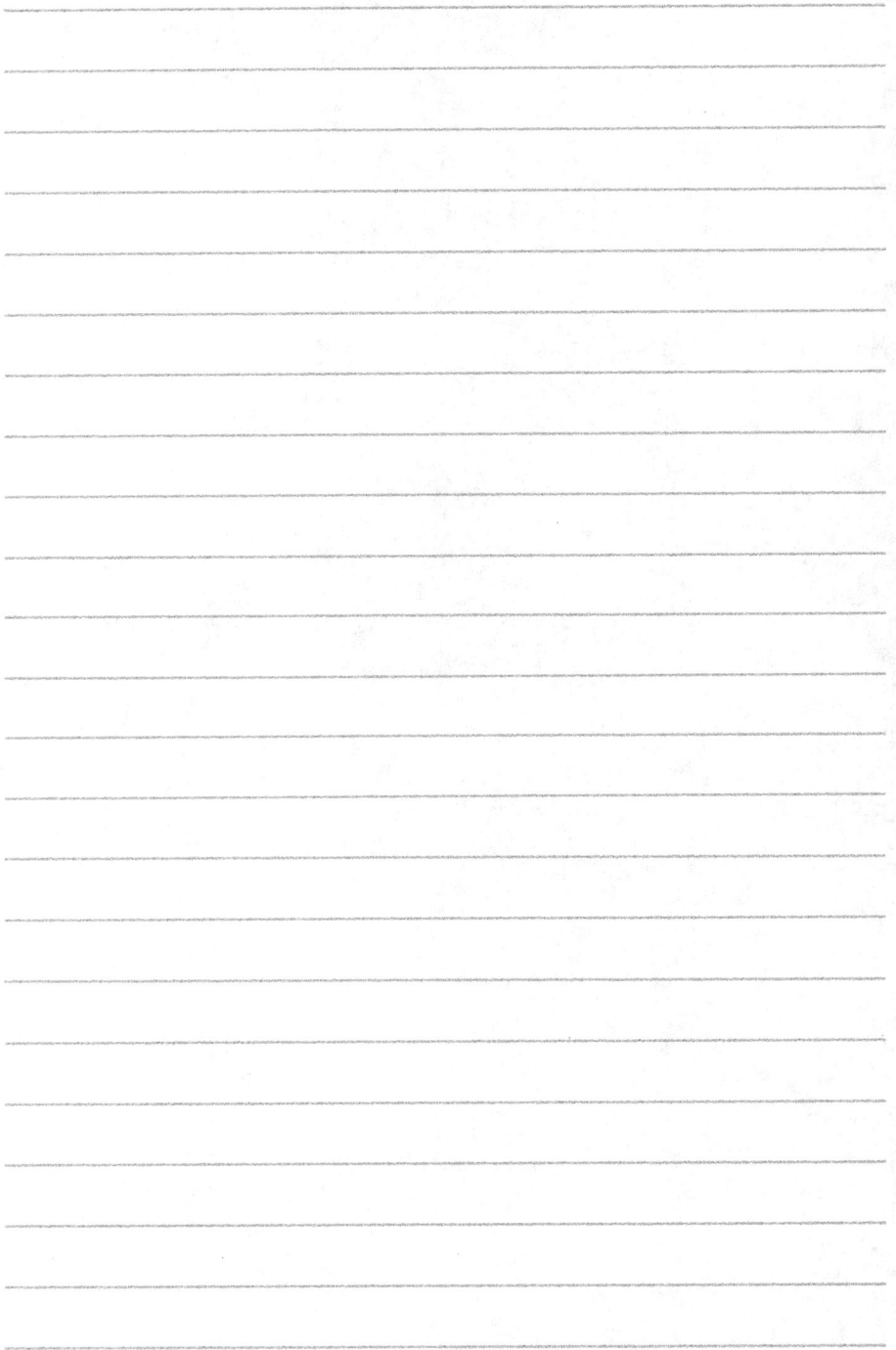

9 RESILIENCE CHECK-IN

A resilient relationship is one with the ability to bounce back again—and again. If you're at a sticking point and wonder whether you can go on, take a look at your internal monologue. Have a discussion with yourself and/or your partner as to how you're encouraging resilience or might be sabotaging your relationship from making any real progress. If you believe you're doing everything listed below and the relationship still isn't moving ahead, you might be on track to figure out how to end, not mend, the relationship. If the latter is relevant, refer to chapter 22, "Compassionate Endings," in *Choices* and/or read through the following steps to see how you can build the staying power in your relationship. Make notes and discuss your reflections with your partner.

9.1 BUILD RESILIENCE

Even if you and your partner report similar feelings or experiences, it doesn't necessarily mean you're both in the same place. Acknowledge what you are doing well (or not so well) to encourage the can-do ability in the relationship. To address the weak links, give a frequency rating by answering never/sometimes/always next to the points below, giving more detail where needed. To gain a full 360 degree view of yourself, invite feedback from your partner and perhaps also from those who know you best. Start with your own feedback about yourself, and be as honest and unedited as possible.

I avoid doomsday thinking and comments such as "here we are again" or "we'll never move past this."

never / sometimes / always

I distinguish between the stuff to challenge and the stuff to let go of.

never / sometimes / always

I can distinguish what belongs in the relationship and what belongs to my past.

never / sometimes / always

I forgive myself and others.

never / sometimes / always

I am able to find meaning in my suffering and I can move on.

never / sometimes / always

I identify and seek what I need in order to heal.

never / sometimes / always

I am prepared to be vulnerable. (Yes, being brave and vulnerable can work in tandem.)

never / sometimes / always

I am patient and determined. Resilience is not gained overnight.

never / sometimes / always

I am prepared to go *through* things rather than get over them.

never / sometimes / always

I am prepared to receive and give honest feedback.

never / sometimes / always

I manage conflict well.

never / sometimes / always

I self soothe.

never / sometimes / always

I am able to lean on my partner when necessary and vice versa.

never / sometimes / always

I am able to stop or get out when resilience turns into negating self-sacrifice.

never / sometimes / always

I don't let relationship set-backs rob me of my self-esteem.

never / sometimes / always

I feel responsible for my partner's feelings.

never / sometimes / always

I take responsibility, rather than dealing out guilt and blame.

never / sometimes / always

I am rational. Your response to set-backs should match the severity of the set-back.

never / sometimes / always

I don't load past set-backs onto current issues.

never / sometimes / always

I set intentions for recovery for the future.

never / sometimes / always

I/we recalibrate often so as to be on the same page and know what threats are lurking.

never / sometimes / always

I value myself as an individual first and in a partnership second. Guard your sense of self: you will always be with you.

never / sometimes / always

I stay true to my innermost values, allowing them to ground me in times of hardship.

never / sometimes / always

I show up and risk failure.

never / sometimes / always

I am proactive in saying sorry, acknowledging when I compromise my own standards, and take action to address the damage done.

never / sometimes / always

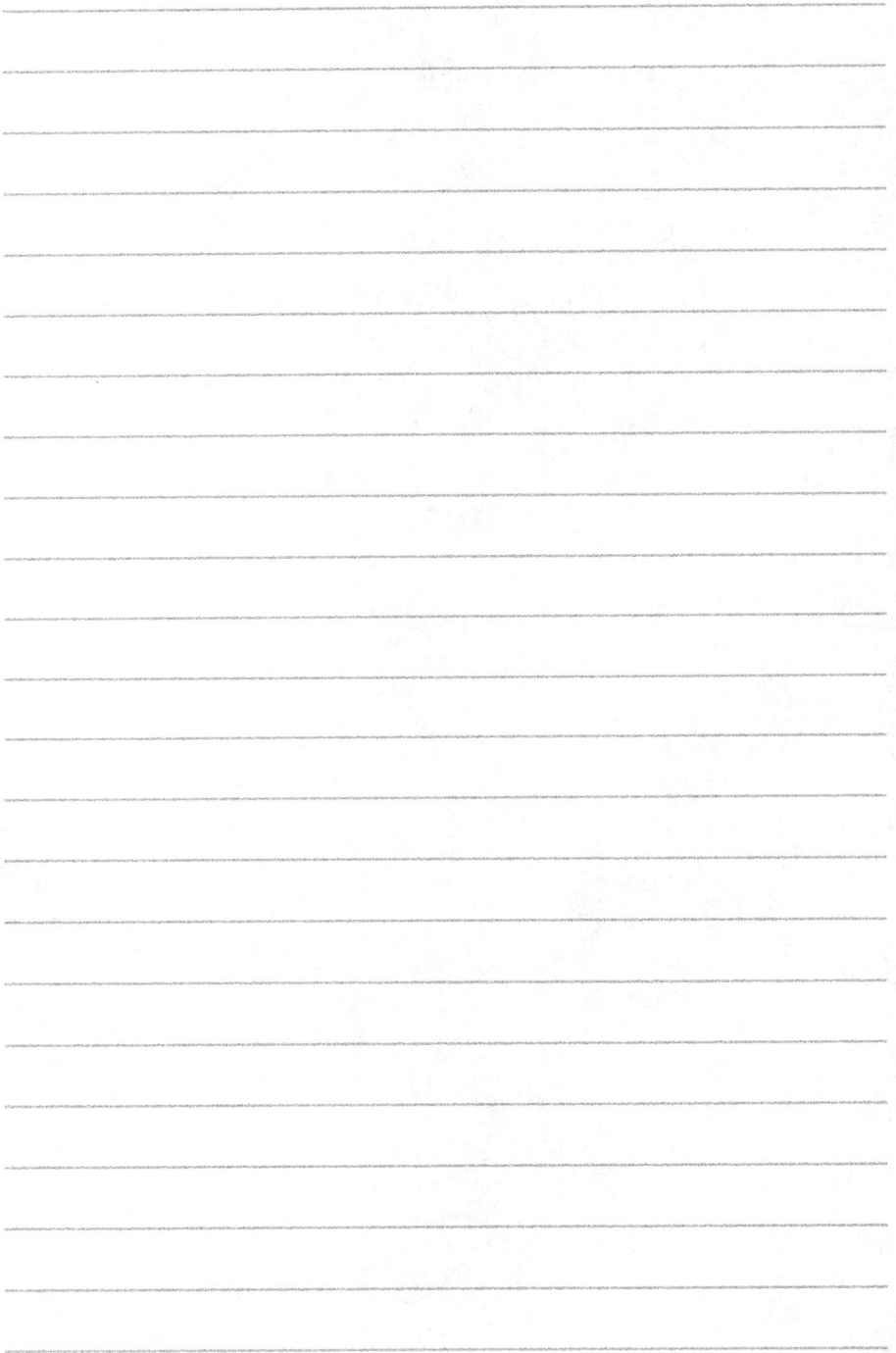

10 CHOOSE RECIPROCITY

The best relationships have a good balance between give and take and where each person contributes equally to maintaining the balance between creativity and function, and between freedom and responsibility. Many couples come for counselling because they're feeling resentful about the burden of too much load, yet often their partner is not aware of the load, real or perceived. Chores and responsibilities can sap all the energy and creativity out of a relationship if they're not managed with an attitude of fairness and equality. Take a look at the following points, give yourself a rating out of 5, where 0 is not at all true and 5 is definitely true, and discuss how each of you reciprocate and what might need to stop, start, or continue.

10.1 HOW TO RECIPROCATE

Taking responsibility. Being self-corrective, saying you're sorry, picking up the ball when you drop it, acknowledging your own and your partner's feelings, verbalizing your expectations.

I rate you: 0 1 2 3 4 5

I rate myself: 0 1 2 3 4 5

Initiating. Employing a proactive and creative work ethic that demonstrates a keen interest in the relationship, whether it's arranging holidays, date nights, or raising discussion points.

I rate you: 0 1 2 3 4 5

I rate myself: 0 1 2 3 4 5

Helping. By being of value in relation to the functions required to service the relationship.

I rate you: 0 1 2 3 4 5

I rate myself: 0 1 2 3 4 5

Participating. By being conscious of what is required and pitching in, whether by listening, taking part in something, or involving yourself.

I rate you: 0 1 2 3 4 5

I rate myself: 0 1 2 3 4 5

Compromising. Accepting the discomfort of not having things all your way but a way that's fair. Owning that choice and ensuring that compromise does not become self-negating martyrdom.

I rate you: 0 1 2 3 4 5

I rate myself: 0 1 2 3 4 5

Connecting. Maintaining the awareness of how the other person is doing emotionally, spiritually, mentally, and physically.

I rate you: 0 1 2 3 4 5

I rate myself: 0 1 2 3 4 5

Exchanging. Setting up a synergistic interdependence by allowing yourself to lean on one another and support one another in a mutually beneficial manner.

I rate you: 0 1 2 3 4 5

I rate myself: 0 1 2 3 4 5

Responding. Being judicious and responsible for the pendulum swing between give and take, ensuring a dynamic motion is maintained and doesn't get stuck, favouring one or none for too long.

I rate you: 0 1 2 3 4 5

I rate myself: 0 1 2 3 4 5

Co-operating. Working in the best interests as set for the relationship by sticking to game plans, agreed boundaries, shared goals, and agreements.

I rate you: 0 1 2 3 4 5

I rate myself: 0 1 2 3 4 5

Receiving. Accepting the offering of the other person with grace and humility.

I rate you: 0 1 2 3 4 5

I rate myself: 0 1 2 3 4 5

Giving. Enjoying your own open-handedness in providing for the other person.

I rate you: 0 1 2 3 4 5

I rate myself: 0 1 2 3 4 5

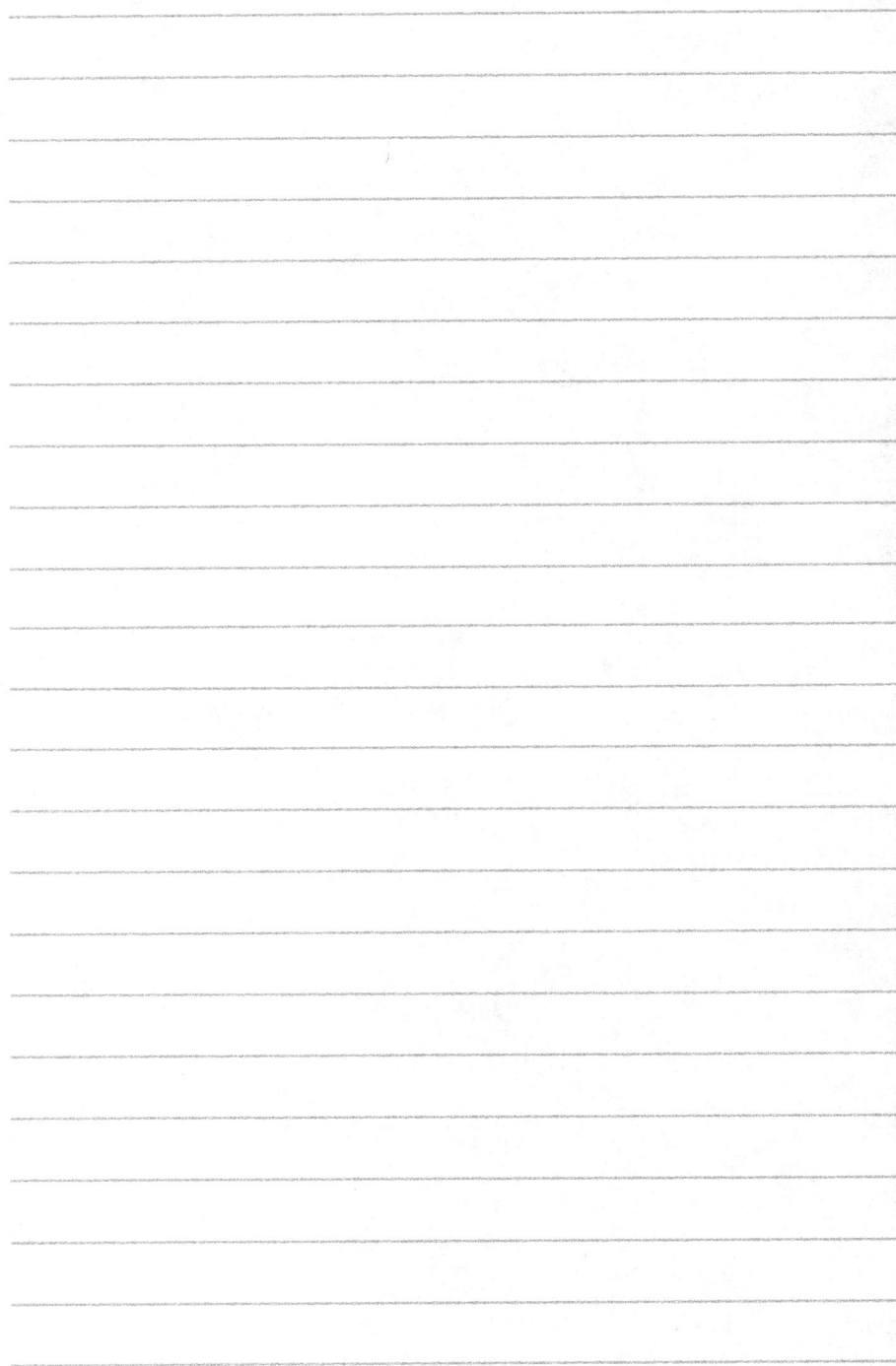

11 CHOOSE RESPONSIBILITY

Responsibility puts us at the wheel of our own lives. The call to take responsibility is really a call to seize our own stuff. When we can be truly accountable for who we are—our thoughts, feelings, and behaviours—then we're well set up to establish healthy bonding patterns with another person. Which means we are not seeking to repair some brokenness in us or them but are prepared to develop a vigorous potential between us. This topic is covered in detail in chapter 18, "Choose Responsibility," of *Choices*.

11.1 DO YOU TAKE RESPONSIBILITY?

Imagine if you were in an interview where the employer was perusing your CV but was only interested in one of your jobs: director of Your Own Life.

Q. As director, you've made some big choices on behalf of yourself. Which choices resulted in tough consequences and which choices resulted in pleasurable consequences? Who's to blame/to thank?

Q. You've been responsible for your personal relationships. How have you gone about selecting partners, and how did those recruits work out? Were you loved well and did you love well? Is your heart safe in your own hands?

Q. You've been managing the health of your self-esteem. Are you competent in backing yourself, soothing yourself, validating and motivating yourself? If not, why not?

Q. You've been in charge of your limits and boundaries. Have you learnt how and when to say no? If not, what—or who—is stopping you?

Q. You've supervised your freedom. Have you allowed yourself too little or too much? If you've been excessive in either direction, how did you benefit from being excessive? Who did you hurt or what did you compromise in the process?

_____

_____

_____

_____

Q. You've reported to yourself. Have you held yourself accountable for failures? How have you acknowledged yourself for achievements? Are you ok with your own fallibility? Have you forgiven yourself, where needed?

_____

_____

_____

_____

Q. You've also been the one in charge of your own physical health. How did you go about deploying those responsibilities? Is your body safe in your hands? Do you value your own energy?

_____

_____

_____

_____

Q. You've been solely responsible for your growth as an adult. What growth have you achieved? Are you where you hoped you would be? If not, what's held you back? What are your goals for advancement?

Q. You are responsible for your own mental health. How have you kept your own levels of stress, anxiety, and depression in check? What do you do to fill your voids and how do your moods, attitudes, optimism, or pessimism affect others?

Q. As you continue as director of Your Own Life going forwards, what footprint have you already left behind? Have you added value to others? Would you employ you for the next stretch? If so, are there any conditions?

11.2 STEPS TO MANIFESTING RESPONSIBILITY IN A RELATIONSHIP

We're drawn to people who take responsibility. It speaks to courage and honesty and gives them a certain presence we instinctively associate with leaders. But this is not about anyone else so focus on you: you and your ability to take the lead in your own life.

Consider whether you employ the following in your relationships and make your comments under each point.

Show respect and honour for your own and each other's history, family, and privacy.

Know what's expected, work to what's expected, and check in to see if what's expected is still relevant.

Keep in touch with your own truth and your partner's truth: Don't be misled by behaviour.

Respond with thoughts, feelings, and deeds that suit mutual wants for support, respect, comfort, care, and love, so as to nourish them, without compromising yourself.

Pitch up with your presence and pitch in with your effort.

Remain conscious as to the fairness and balance between you regarding obligations and independences, novelties, and tasks.

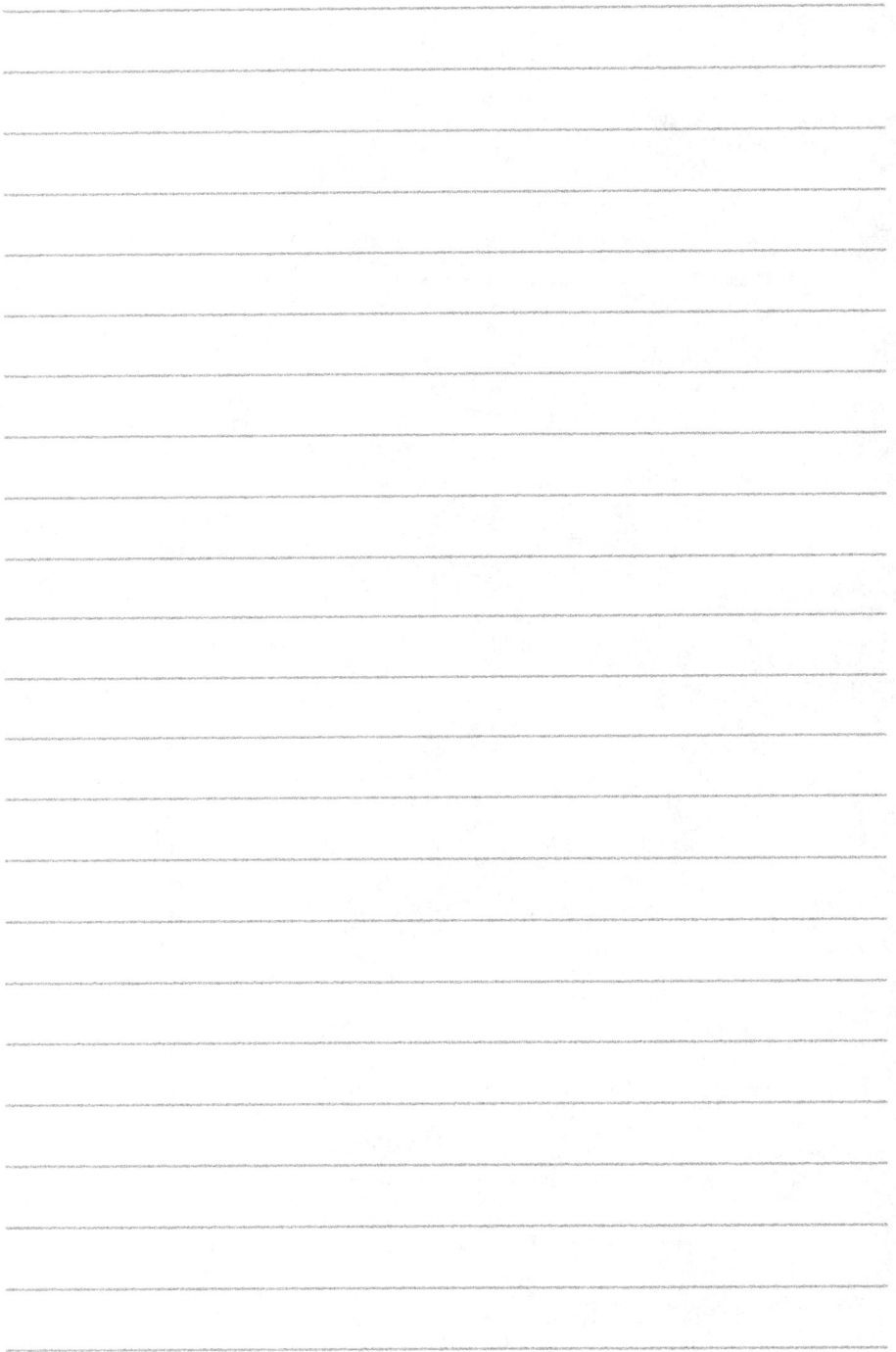

12 CHOOSE FRIENDSHIP

In chapter 19, "Choose Friendship," of *Choices* I discuss that relevance, realness, and empathy are key to maintaining a friendship, and recalibrating these three is essential if we're to stay on the same page. This exercise looks at empathy in particular because it's the one aspect of friendship that frequently gets tossed aside, and it's the one quality that can keep us truly connected. This is an exercise in reflection that might help you nudge yourself into pitching up with more heart.

12.1 IMPROVE YOUR EMPATHY

If you've been told you lack empathy, or if you want to up your empathy game, here's how.

- Place yourself in the shoes of your inner child and ask that part of you where there are feelings such as withdrawal, sadness, not feeling good enough, hurt, loneliness, resentment, or anger. And ask your younger self what you need more of to make you feel happy, spontaneous, playful, trusting, safe, and carefree. Empathise with your inner little you if you want to offer authentic empathy to someone else.
- Listen. Listen. Listen.
- Demonstrate empathy with facial expressions that respond to the person's story.
- Drop your tone and volume to create intimacy.
- Trust your intuition as to when it's good timing to reach out to touch someone—a hug for containment, an arm-rub or a back pat to soothe, a firm kiss on the cheek on parting for support and encouragement. And know when it's time to stop so as not to become awkward.

- Empathy is communicated in the small things. A wink can say "don't sweat this," a sigh can signal you feel their burden, eyes widening echo shock, a smile and a nod encourages someone to continue, placing your hand on your heart signals you feel for their heart.
- Reflecting their emotions and verbalizing yours creates a real heart-to-heart cause-and-effect type moment, e.g., "your happiness fills me with joy," or, "I feel inspired by your brave-heartedness," or, "my stomach knots when I see you in such pain."
- Empathy is not pity and it is not about rescuing someone. Empathy is the ability to *feel with* and offer a sense of family and understanding to a person, animal, and all living things—without needing to sacrifice yourself at the same time.

NOTES

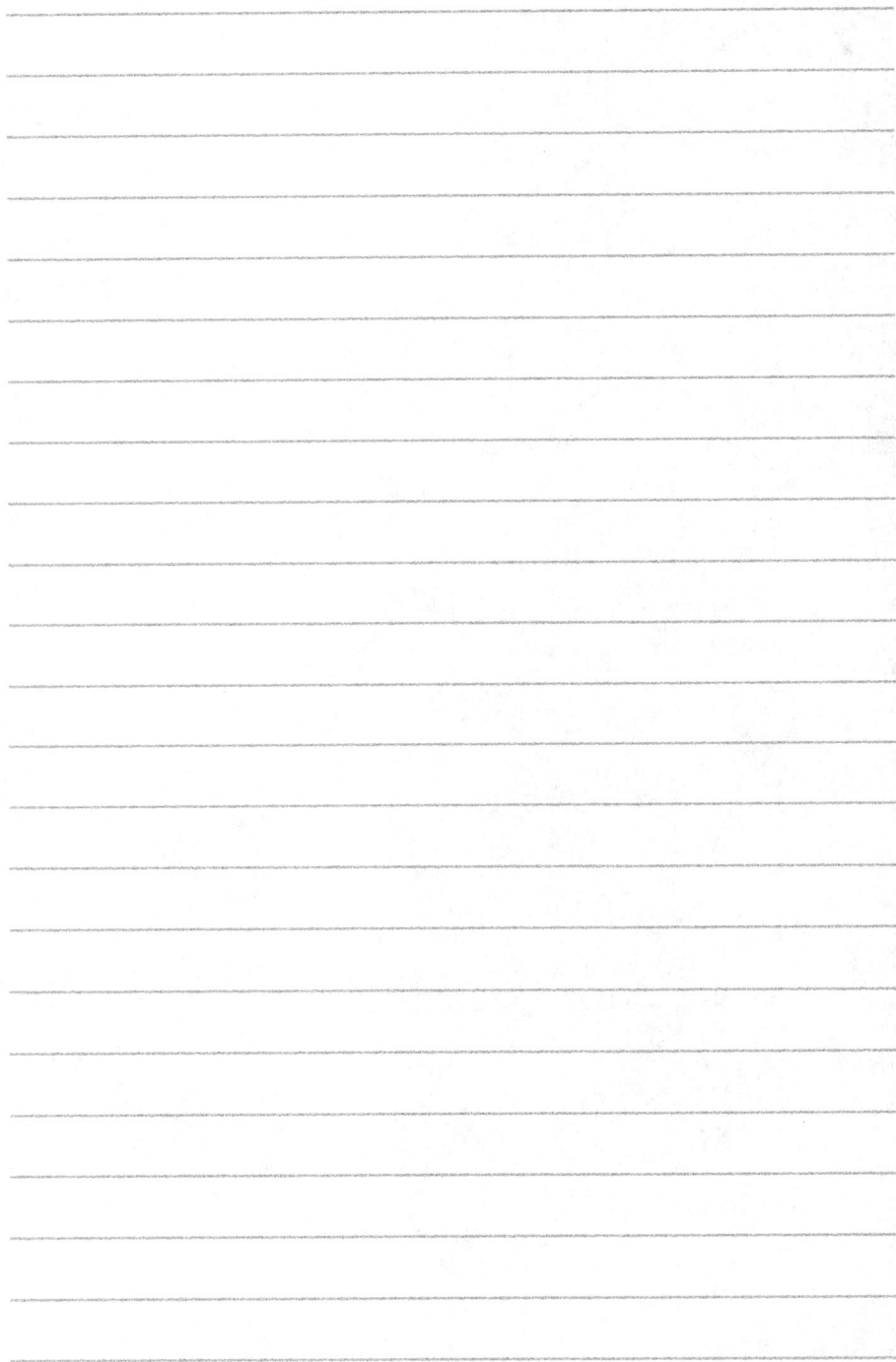

13 CHOOSE PASSION

The level of passion shared between two people and the degree to which they still want and desire each other is a valuable barometer on how the relationship is doing. Keep updated as to your partner's desires and getting out of your comfort zone. It is key to keeping your sex life fresh, playful, and exciting. This is another master choice, and igniting your passion will have you securing the relationship again versus risking the relationship when it becomes boring, tired, and lack-lustre.

To prepare for this exercise, make sure you each have a copy of the questionnaire. Complete the questionnaire in your own time, taking your time to think about and explore the questions. Then set up a date night with your partner and nudge yourself to be romantic and creative about the date—think music, lighting, privacy...

Accept that you might feel awkward and shy about your answers, but push through to share and discuss each question. Go in with an open heart and mind, and don't judge your partner's answers. Remember you will both feel vulnerable and exposed, but disclosure begets disclosure. Confirm that this sharing will be kept safe and confidential, and let the night take you where it and you want it to. Enjoy!

RESTRAINTS: I TEND TO AVOID SEX WHEN...

You or I use or bring our tech (phones/laptop) to bed	**yes / no**
When we have watched TV in bed beforehand	**yes / no**
The children/our parents/visitors are in the next room	**yes / no**
We have discussed certain topics that are passion killers	**yes / no**
I am tired/you are tired	**yes / no**

I am stressed or worried/you are stressed or worried	**yes / no**
When it feels like a chore/too much effort	**yes / no**
I feel unattractive	**yes / no**
I feel unnoticed	**yes / no**
I assume you don't want sex right now	**yes / no**
I fear being rejected or risk feeling inadequate/you fear being rejected or risk feeling inadequate	**yes / no**
I haven't bathed/you haven't bathed	**yes / no**
I feel disconnected from you	**yes / no**
I've/you've taken stimulants (alcohol/drugs)	**yes / no**
There's a risk of being disturbed or discovered	**yes / no**
Everything's not "perfect"	**yes / no**
Or when (give detail) …	**yes / no**

CAN BE AROUSED BY...

You flirting with me	0 1 2 3 4 5
General discussion about sex	0 1 2 3 4 5
Dirty talk about sex	0 1 2 3 4 5
You telling me what you want to do to me sexually	0 1 2 3 4 5
Sexual imagery, e.g. pornography, live sex shows, explicit photographs	0 1 2 3 4 5
Watching you arouse yourself	0 1 2 3 4 5
Reading erotica	0 1 2 3 4 5
You narrating erotica to me	0 1 2 3 4 5
You telling me about your fantasies	0 1 2 3 4 5

Seeing you naked	0 1 2 3 4 5
You watching me when I am naked	0 1 2 3 4 5
Being in certain places, such as...	0 1 2 3 4 5
Watching you move (dance, walk, exercise)	0 1 2 3 4 5
Feeling your skin/body against mine	0 1 2 3 4 5
Smelling your scent	0 1 2 3 4 5
You teasing me and delaying gratification	0 1 2 3 4 5
When you reach orgasm	0 1 2 3 4 5
Watching you with other people	0 1 2 3 4 5
Seeing you in different outfits	0 1 2 3 4 5
You reaching an orgasm each time is important	0 1 2 3 4 5
Me reaching an orgasm each time is important	0 1 2 3 4 5

The most arousing part of your body for me is...

_____

_____

_____

The sexual position that gives me most pleasure is...

_____

_____

_____

_____

WHEN YOU TOUCH ME, I PREFER...

Nipples   0 1 2 3 4 5

Spine   0 1 2 3 4 5

Elbows   0 1 2 3 4 5

Collar bone   0 1 2 3 4 5

Forearms   0 1 2 3 4 5

Neck   0 1 2 3 4 5

Belly button   0 1 2 3 4 5

Hair   0 1 2 3 4 5

Shoulders   0 1 2 3 4 5

Hands   0 1 2 3 4 5

Tummy   0 1 2 3 4 5

Wrists   0 1 2 3 4 5

Mouth   0 1 2 3 4 5

Pubic bone   0 1 2 3 4 5

Tongue   0 1 2 3 4 5

Anus—inner/outer   0 1 2 3 4 5

Face   0 1 2 3 4 5

Vagina—inner/outer   0 1 2 3 4 5

Skin   0 1 2 3 4 5

Perineum   0 1 2 3 4 5

Legs   0 1 2 3 4 5

Labia   0 1 2 3 4 5

Inner thighs	0 1 2 3 4 5
Clitoris	0 1 2 3 4 5
Hips	0 1 2 3 4 5
Penis	0 1 2 3 4 5
Feet	0 1 2 3 4 5
Testicles	0 1 2 3 4 5
Groin	0 1 2 3 4 5
Bum cheeks	0 1 2 3 4 5
Upper back	0 1 2 3 4 5
Lower back	0 1 2 3 4 5
Ears	0 1 2 3 4 5

I FIND I GET MOST AROUSED WHEN...

You take control	yes / no
I take control	yes / no
We take turns	yes / no
Control is not a factor	yes / no

My idea of you taking control is...

_____

_____

_____

_____

My idea of me taking control is…

A fantasy I have that involves control (or submission) is…

Another fantasy I have that doesn't involve control (or submission) is…

A taboo that arouses me is…

WHEN IT COMES TO HOW YOU TOUCH ME, I ENJOY...

Stroking	0 1 2 3 4 5
Tickling	0 1 2 3 4 5
Massage	0 1 2 3 4 5
Kissing	0 1 2 3 4 5
Licking	0 1 2 3 4 5
Biting	0 1 2 3 4 5
Smacking	0 1 2 3 4 5
Blowing	0 1 2 3 4 5
Sucking	0 1 2 3 4 5

I LIKE THE WAY YOU TOUCH ME TO BE...

Gentle	0 1 2 3 4 5
Firm	0 1 2 3 4 5
Rough	0 1 2 3 4 5
Unpredictable	0 1 2 3 4 5
Virtual	0 1 2 3 4 5

ATTITUDE

I think sex is important to you	0 1 2 3 4 5
Sex is important to me	0 1 2 3 4 5
I feel closer to you when we make love often	0 1 2 3 4 5
I think you find me desirable	0 1 2 3 4 5
I think I am desirable	0 1 2 3 4 5

I know what arouses me	0 1 2 3 4 5
I know what arouses you	0 1 2 3 4 5
I like it when you tell me what to do to you	0 1 2 3 4 5
I like to tell you what to do to me	0 1 2 3 4 5
It's important for me that you initiate sex	0 1 2 3 4 5
I don't take it personally if you don't want to have sex	0 1 2 3 4 5
I am open to experimenting with sexual toys and stimulants	0 1 2 3 4 5
I am able to say "no" when you want something that crosses my boundaries	0 1 2 3 4 5
I feel confident enough in myself to be able to share my innermost desires with you	0 1 2 3 4 5
I trust you enough to be able to share my innermost desires with you	0 1 2 3 4 5
I think our sex life is boring	0 1 2 3 4 5
I prefer your body/genitals to be hairless	0 1 2 3 4 5
Romantic gestures are important to me	0 1 2 3 4 5

Some ideas of romantic gestures that work for me are:

_____

_____

_____

_____

_____

My idea of ideal sexual frequency is _____ per week / month / year.

The best sexual memory I have of us is...

_____

_____

_____

The reason the above memory was so good for me is...

_____

_____

_____

When making love, I would like you to do less...

_____

_____

_____

When making love, I would like you to do more...

_____

_____

_____

_____

Time of day/night that I prefer making love...

_____

_____

_____

_____

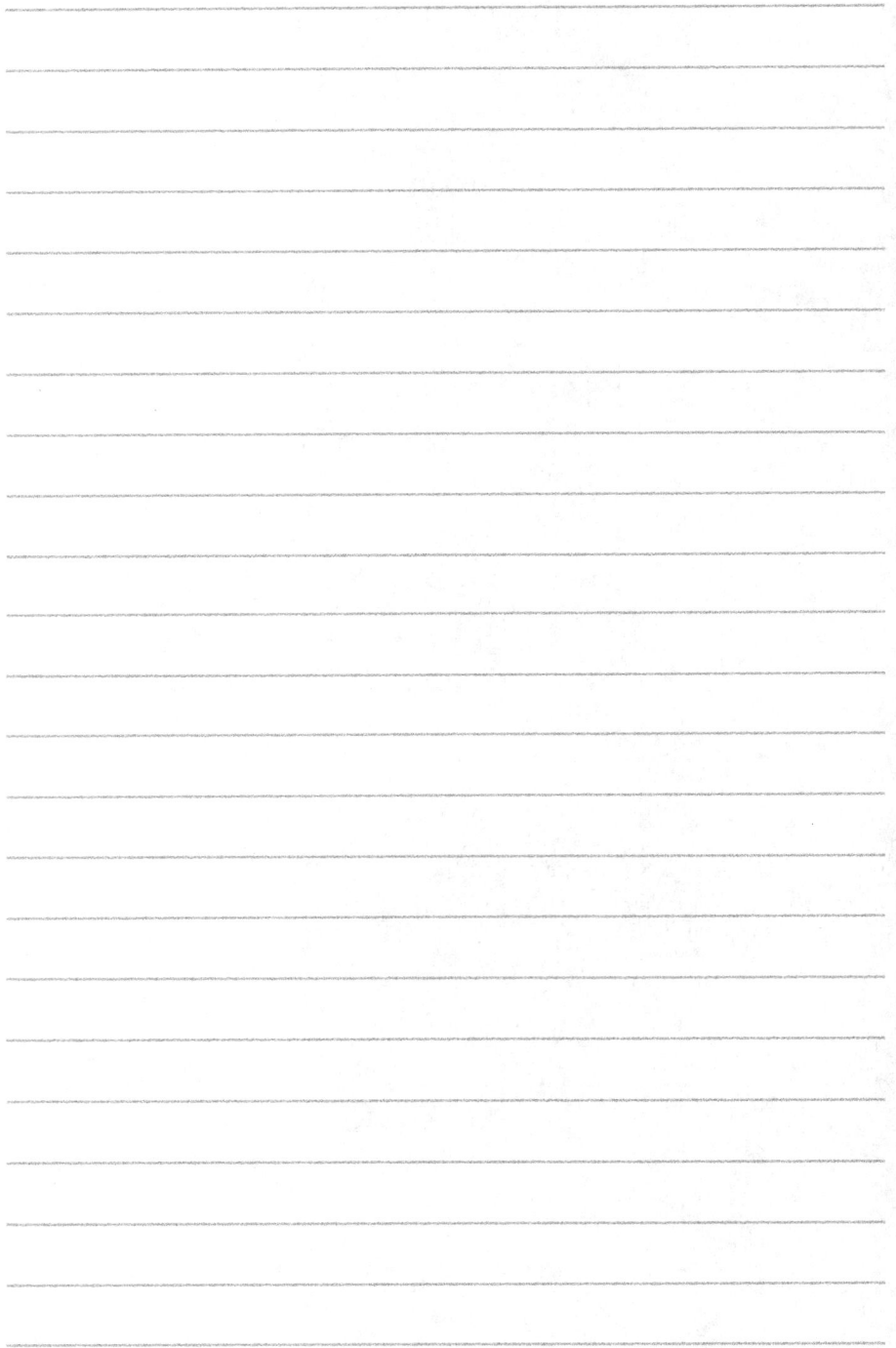

14 CHOOSE BELIEF

Refer to chapter 21, "Choose Belief," in *Choices* and you'll see that sometimes, as happened to me in my relationships, we're all out of trust, respect is low, and hope is waning—the relationship is in trauma. Yet somehow we find the wherewithal to persevere. That might be due to the belief we have in the relationship and in the other person.

Belief is a relationship's mojo—the intangible *something* that allows us to hold on. But when it's gone, it's so very difficult to rekindle. If you're in a relationship that feels like it's hanging on by the short and curlies, and you want to renew belief, follow these steps. You might find that you can garner just enough reserve fuel to do the work, perhaps through therapy, that would be required to mend the relationship (or be reconciled that it needs to end).

14.1 REKINDLE THE MOJO IN YOUR RELATIONSHIP

Make notes between each point below to help your access where you are at in the relationship and to help you find out what's missing. Share this exercise with your partner and ask them to do the same. Then sit down in a quiet place and share your answers with each other.

Think about what you believed in when you set out and what you believe now.

Reflect on how much was fantasy and what could have/might still be achieved.

Be real with the other person and reveal the thoughts and feelings that are attached to your belief system.

Share the enduring qualities that have you believing in yourself and the other person.

_____

_____

_____

_____

_____

_____

Share the qualities in you that you'd like them to support.

_____

_____

_____

_____

_____

_____

Ask for feedback as to where they might have lost belief in you/the relationship.

_____

_____

_____

_____

Give feedback as where you might have lost belief in them/the relationship.

If you believed in yourself, your partner, and the relationship, what difference would it make to your life?

Finally, give yourself time to build belief, for unlike the immediate gratification of enchantment, belief is an accumulated quality.

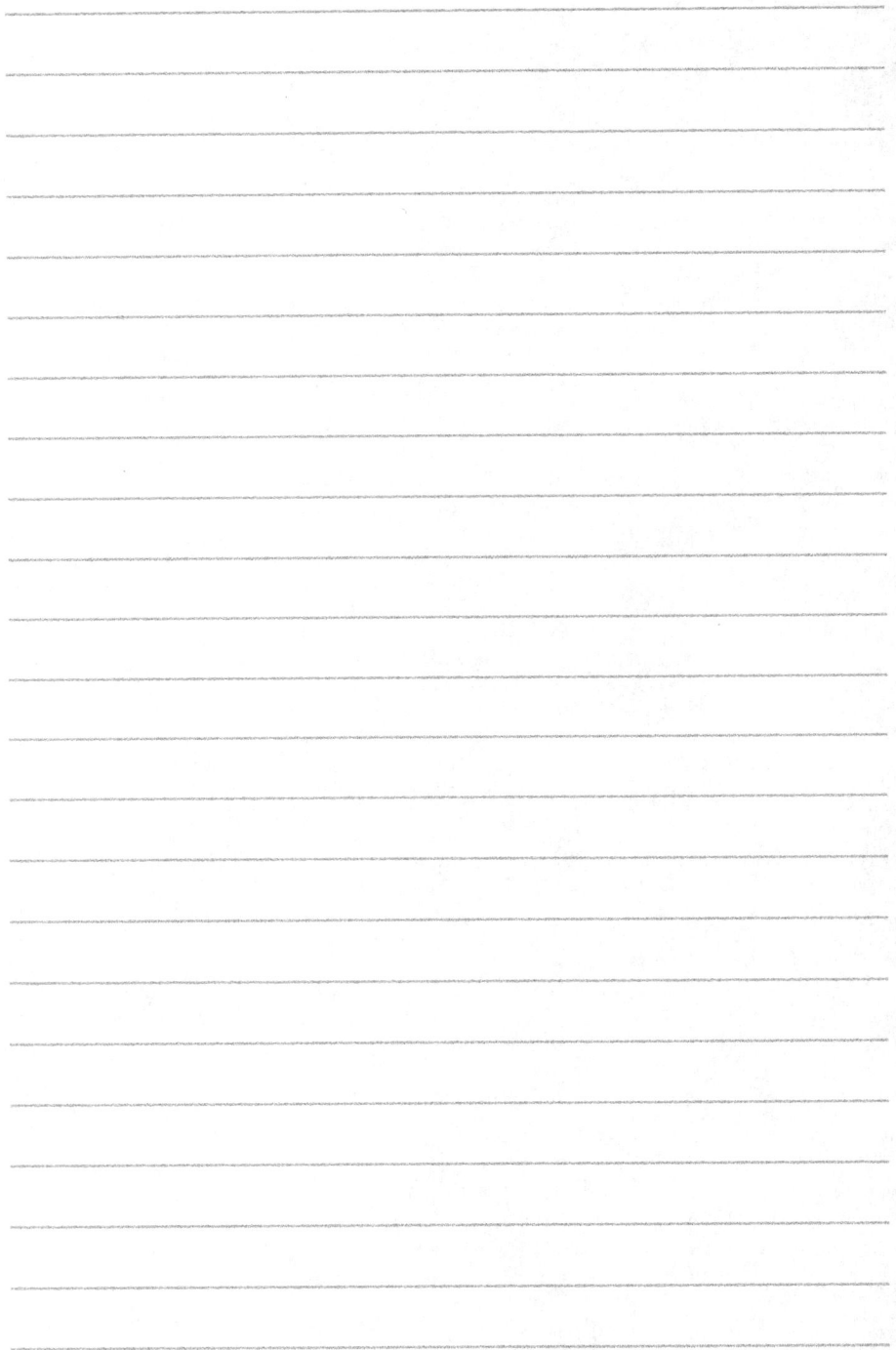

15 COMPASSIONATE ENDINGS

The end of every relationship generates pain, but knowing the love is gone is an easier position than the far tougher dilemma of loving someone but not wanting to be with them any longer.

It feels counter-intuitive to end a relationship with someone you love. Elusive, niggling rumblings in your gut meet with guilt every time thoughts of leaving arise.

15.1 IS YOUR RELATIONSHIP IN SERIOUS TROUBLE?

If you know that you have tried your best to give your relationship a chance but it still feels like you are losing self esteem or that you are not able to be yourself, it might be time to end it rather than mend it. There is no shame in calling time on a relationship that's run its course.

Take a critical look at your relationship's health by considering the following exercise. A relationship that's coming to an end has several cues—note how many times you say "yes" to these statements.

You avoid spending time together.	**yes / no**
You feel controlled and have insufficient freedom.	**yes / no**
You don't like or respect one another anymore.	**yes / no**
Your values are not aligned.	**yes / no**
You don't like who you are when you're with your partner.	**yes / no**

Jealousy, insecurity, and mistrust are dominant feelings.	**yes / no**
There is emotional and/or physical abuse.	**yes / no**
It feels like you are on a roller coaster ride.	**yes / no**
It's as if your partner is in control of your self-esteem.	**yes / no**
You can't be yourself or don't know who you are anymore.	**yes / no**
Your conflict frequently results in the entire relationship being threatened.	**yes / no**
You seldom make love.	**yes / no**
Your realistic wants are not being met.	**yes / no**
You find yourself being attracted to other men/women.	**yes / no**
You struggle to communicate about important matters.	**yes / no**
Your partner is more like a sibling or best friend than a life companion and lover.	**yes / no**

15.2 FAREWELL FAILURE, HELLO CLOSURE – KNOW YOUR REASONS WHY

For many people, ending and leaving a relationship is one of the hardest choices they have or will ever make. If you've done this before, you might recall being paralysed by guilt and doubt or fear that you might be making the wrong choice and could regret it later. Questions like "what if you'll always be alone?" "What if this was the best relationship you could ever have and your expectations for a more fulfilling relationship are unrealistic?" "What if you're just blowing things out of proportion and things were not so bad that you had to end it?"

Or you might be confused by how much your partner reels when you end it, doing anything to get you back—their desperate feelings might start to replace your feelings of certainty and you might find yourself wanting to end their pain by simply staying. This is where your "why?" for ending the relationship is so essential. To get to your why and to ensure you don't have regrets, acknowledge both the dark and the light of the relationship. Contemplate the time you shared, using photographs to prompt your memory if need be. Then make journal entries to help you prepare to speak to your partner, using the prompts below. For more on this topic refer to chapter 22 in *Choices*.

15.3 CLOSURE EXERCISE

When I think through the chapters of our story together, I want you to know that...

_____

_____

_____

_____

_____

_____

_____

Some of the most meaningful memories I have of you as an individual are...

_____

_____

_____

_____

_____

_____

_____

_____

_____

Some of the most meaningful memories I have of our time together as a couple are...

However, I won't miss...

But I will miss...

I realise I could have managed our relationship better by...

I believe you could have managed our relationship better by...

I need to forgive you for...

I need to forgive myself for...

The hardest part about letting you go is...(or would be if you have not reached a conclusion)

I know that our time together has reached its end because...

Thanks to our relationship, I have learnt the following about myself...

I wish for you the following as you move forward in life...

_____

_____

_____

_____

_____

_____

_____

_____

_____

When the time comes to share your script with your partner, I recommend that you choose a quiet place, allow plenty of time for recovery thereafter, expect that it will be very challenging so have tissues on hand, self-soothe throughout the exercise, and pace yourself.

If both parties have prepared for the exercise (recommended), I find that doing one answer at a time with each of you exchanging your answers for each point is best as it allows for you to gather yourself and to really listen to what your partner is saying. It also helps you stay in sync with one another. Remember you can adlib and expand on your journal entries. The idea is to be prepared whilst being yourself and pitching up in the moment.

Finally, keep reminding yourself that you are giving the relationship dignity by honouring the relationship's journey. Trust that truth-telling will ground you and that when the pain has passed, you will be grateful for having been true to yourself.

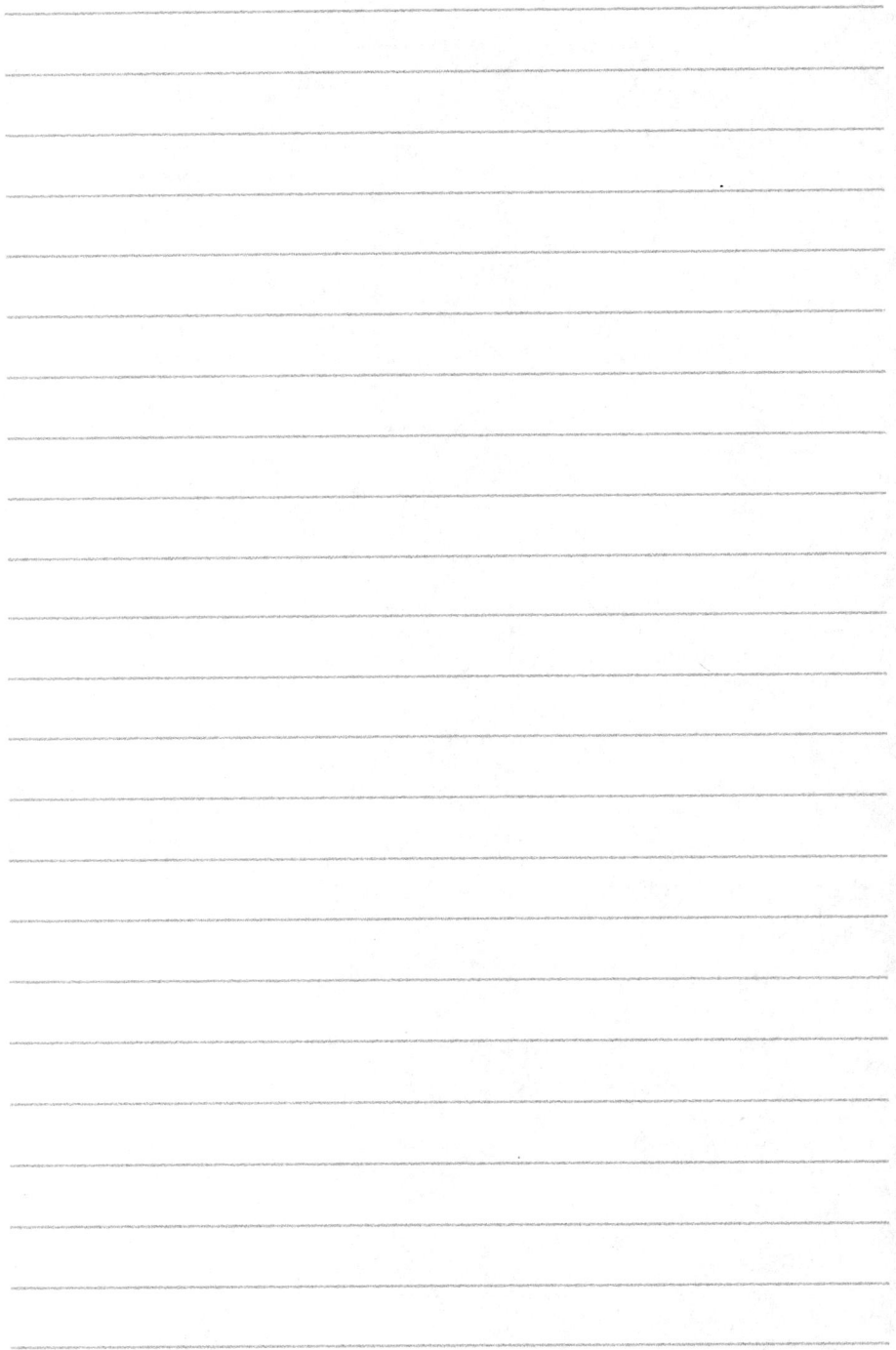

16 LOVE: TRULY THE END GAME

This final exercise should help raise your awareness of your own take on love and its role in your relationships. It's these relationships that will have determined your level of self-esteem and, therefore, your openness to giving and receiving love. Whether your children, parents, siblings, friends, former lovers, or spouse, they have provided multiple reflections to give you a gauge on your safety levels in love, how adequate you feel in your love, and how *wanted* you are.

Here's a final exercise to help you identify where you are right now with regards to love and to establish the work that is yet to be done. As you prepare for this exercise, bring into your mind's eye the key people who matter most to you.

16.1 LOVE AS MY LIFE'S BAROMETER

Regardless of the state of these relationships right now, these are the people in my life who I *know* I love:

_____

_____

_____

_____

_____

_____

_____

I expect the following people would be surprised at how much I love them:

What holds me back from showing loved ones a true reflection of my love is:

I least like who I am when I am with the following people:

The following unwanted qualities come up in me when I am relating to that person/those people (as mentioned above):

If I could accept/forgive/let go of my judgment towards myself with regards to the above unwanted qualities, can I see myself being able to express my love more freely, sincerely, or differently? Elaborate.

If my life had to end right now, what positive statements do I fear my loved ones would not be able to say about me yet?

When my life ends, to know I have loved well, these are the specific memories I want my loved ones to have of me:

Considering what I am doing right now and what I wish to be to my loved ones, these four things are what I would need to do differently to have a loving opinion of myself and to show my love in ways that matter:

These are the people in my life who I appreciate for reflecting that I am loved:

_____

_____

_____

_____

_____

_____

_____

_____

We are likely to love best where we feel wanted, but often it's the people who reject us that teach us most about the meaning of love. Sometimes we have to lose their love in order to learn how to love without controlling, without needing to be needed, and without guarantees. Ultimately all the people we attract to our lives show us who we actually are and who we are not. They are our greatest, most meaningful mirrors.

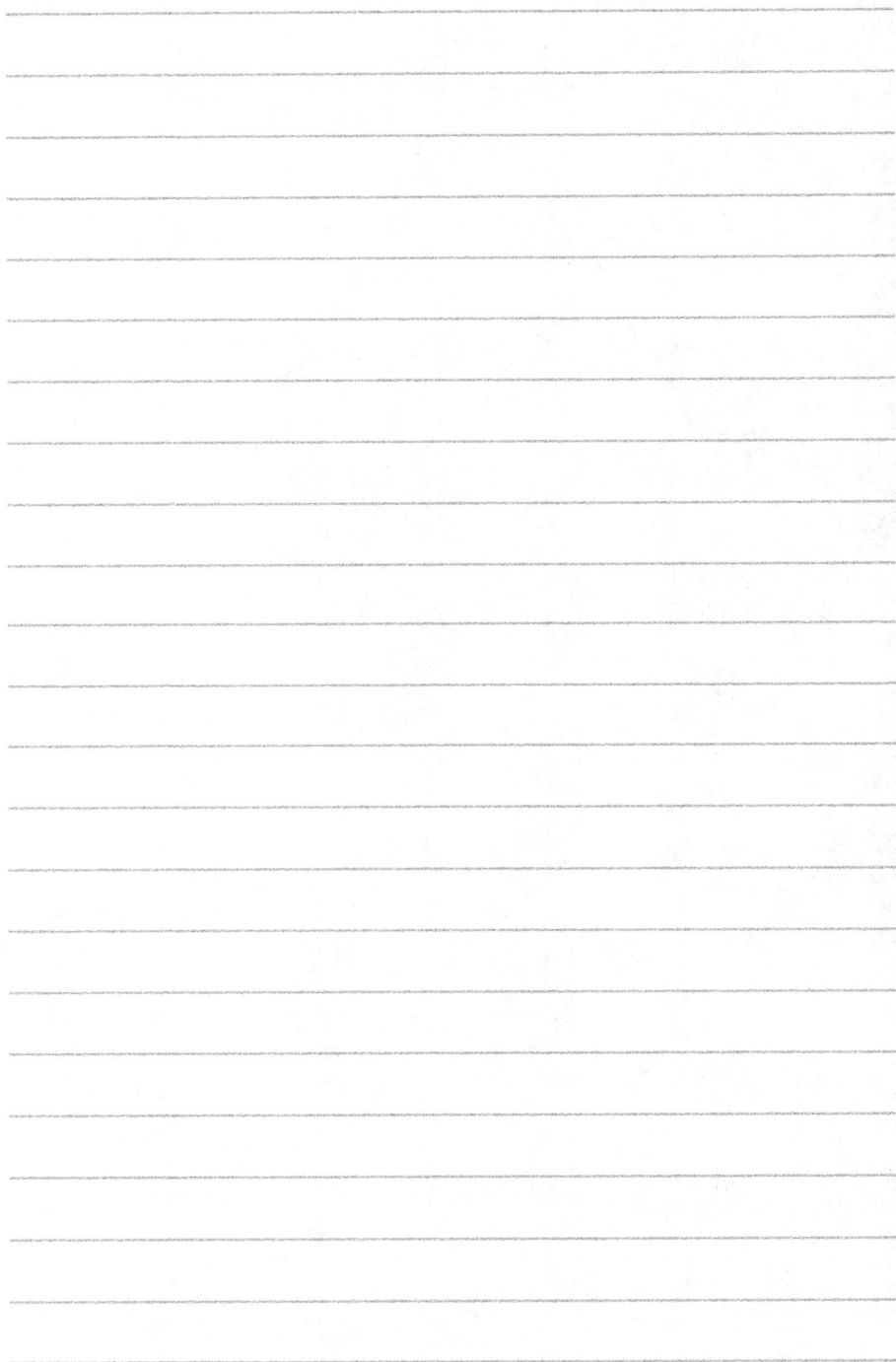

We recommend taking *Choices*
(and this companion workbook)
to your book club.

Get your reader's guide for
book club discussion questions here:
ingeniumbooks.com/choices-book-club